THE ART OF
JEWELLERY DESIGN
FROM IDEA TO REALITY

THE ART OF
JEWELLERY DESIGN
FROM IDEA TO REALITY

ELIZABETH OLVER

A&C Black • London

A QUARTO BOOK

First published in the United Kingdom in 2002
by A & C Black (Publishers) Limited
35 Bedford Row, London WCIR 4JH

ISBN 0-7136-6155-0

QUAR.AJD

Conceived, designed, and produced by
Quarto Publishing plc
The Old Brewery
6 Blundell Street
London N7 9BH

Project editor Marie-Claire Muir
Senior art editor Penny Cobb
Art editor/designer Jill Mumford
Photographer Paul Forester
Picture researcher Yvonne Kulagowski
Copy editor Ian Kearey
Proofreader Claire Waite Brown
Indexer Pamella Ellis

Art director Moira Clinch
Publisher Piers Spence

Manufactured by Universal Graphics Pte Ltd.,
Singapore

Printed by Leefung-Asco- Printers Ltd, China

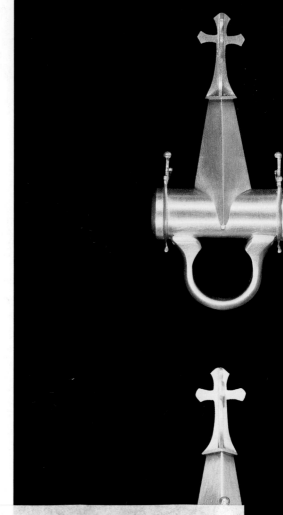

CONTENTS

INTRODUCTION 6

ESSENTIAL DESIGN TOOLS 8
drawing ability 10
sketchbook 12
visual journal 14
technical journal 16
craft skills 18

STAGES OF THE DESIGN PROCESS 20
design development 22
inspiration 26
sketching 30
design brief 32
concept 34
brainstorming 36
research 38
samples and test pieces 40
model making 42
fabrication 44

ELEMENTS OF DESIGN 46
shape 48
form 54
texture 60
colour 66
the five senses 72
emotion 76
function 80
materials 84
processes 90

CREATIVE CONCEPTS 96
organic 98
geometric 104
abstract 108
figurative 114
narrative 118
symbolic 122
icons 128
fashion 134
fine 138
series 144
sculptural 150

GLOSSARY 156

INDEX 158

CREDITS 160

introduction

My enthusiasm and love for jewellery began many years ago when I was still at school, and continued to grow as I studied jewellery making and design at London's Central School of Art and Design. Through running my own business, designing and making fashion and fine jewellery, I learned about jewellery design in a more specific context, which helped me to understand and appreciate jewellery from a different, and perhaps more grounded perspective.

Through a second degree at the Royal College of Art, and teaching at the Central School of Art and Design as senior lecturer, I learned more about the complexity and wonder of jewellery design. After many hours designing, making, and deliberating with the wise and the good, I came to realise that, as in other areas of life, there is much that we take for granted, and that there is more to jewellery than meets the eye. Take, for example, the materials we normally

with good design, an ounce of gold can be made to be worth twice its original value

associate with the discipline, and you could be forgiven for assuming that precious materials are what make jewellery so special. Actually, it is the design that distinguishes one piece of gold from another — and with good design, an ounce of gold can be made to be worth twice its original value.

During many conversations with would-be designers, I noted with interest that while most of them want to design beautiful jewellery, few actually realise how difficult that is to achieve. After all, if it were so easy to make something beautiful everyone would be doing it effortlessly, but alas, it is easier said than done. We may know instinctively what is beautiful, but creating a thing of beauty is another matter. To cook fine food, you need to understand what tastes good, and how texture, colour and flavour can be combined to produce something that is exciting and appetising to the palate and eye. As with fine cuisine, interesting and beautiful jewellery is easier to appreciate than create.

Jewellery design requires a healthy curiosity and appetite for understanding

Understanding what we like and dislike about our visual, tactile, sensual, and functional world is essential to the design process, and is an exciting learning experience. It provides a designer with a personal perspective necessary to give character to a design. Personality is what distinguishes design and saves it from being just another eternal, anonymous, eclectic repeat; it makes a design noteworthy, exciting, provocative, distinctive, and individual.

Jewellery design requires a healthy curiosity and appetite for understanding and enjoying design 'ingredients'. I hope this book will both satisfy and expand that appetite, and that it will provide aspiring designers with guidance, ideas and inspiration in order to create unexpected, exciting and exquisite jewellery. To that end, I am particularly delighted to be able to showcase innovative work from contemporary international jewellery designers — many of them well-established in the field, others newcomers who are pushing the boundaries of jewellery design.

Learning how to design jewellery can be easy, it can be incredibly enjoyable and exhilarating, it can be a challenge and it can be a frustration, but most of all it can be a wonderful journey that has the potential to enrich your life!

Elizabeth Olver

how to use this book

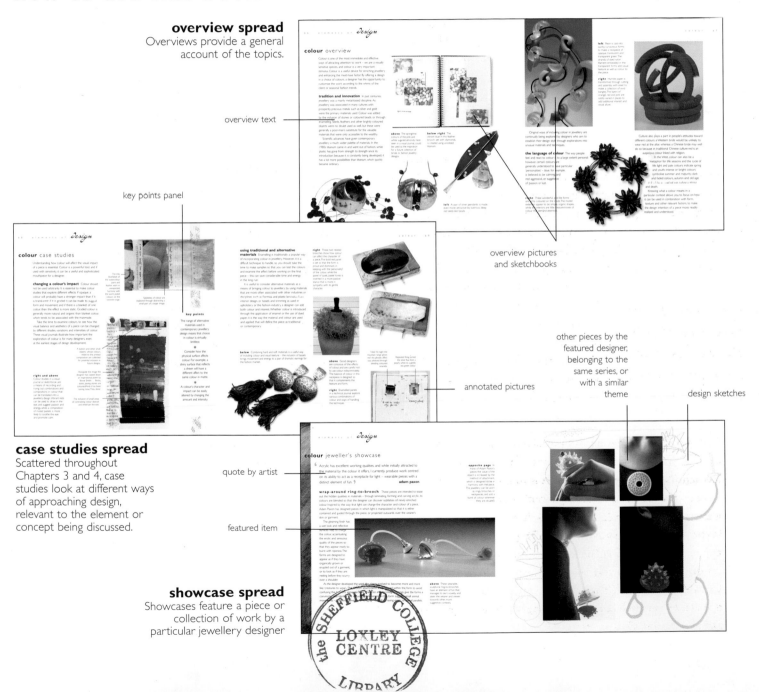

overview spread
Overviews provide a general account of the topics.

overview text

key points panel

overview pictures and sketchbooks

case studies spread
Scattered throughout Chapters 3 and 4, case studies look at different ways of approaching design, relevant to the element or concept being discussed.

quote by artist

featured item

other pieces by the featured designer, belonging to the same series, or with a similar theme

design sketches

annotated pictures

showcase spread
Showcases feature a piece or collection of work by a particular jewellery designer

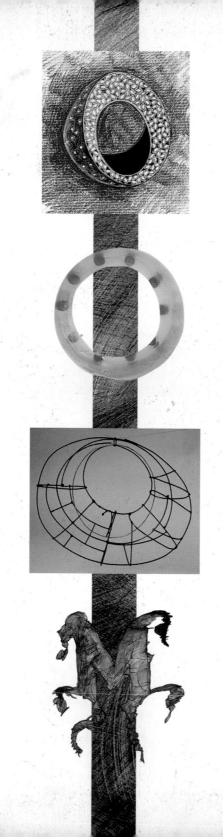

CHAPTER ONE
ESSENTIAL DESIGN TOOLS

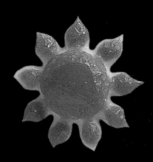

There are a few indispensable tools that are needed to design jewellery, but how a person approaches design will differ from one person to another and the relevance and importance of the tools will be weighted accordingly.

For some, design will be an extension of their love of the physical act of crafting, so craft skills and the technical journal may form the cornerstones of their design process. For others, the yearning to design may stem from a desire to express something that inspires them in a beautiful and unique jewellery form, and they may not feel the need to develop craft skills.

Whatever your approach, ultimately the essential tools needed for jewellery design are enthusiasm and commitment.

drawing ability

Jewellery design may not require innate and exceptional drawing talent, but whether for themselves or others, a designer will inevitably need to describe an object, a subject or a making process using two-dimensional visual images.

communication and learning Drawing is a skill that is virtually indispensable in jewellery design. It is an essential tool of communication and is used at every stage of the design development process. At the initial stages of design, drawings are used mainly to record inspiration, experiment with variations, carry out research and visualise ideas. At a more practical level, designers often illustrate technical aspects through drawings to aid in decision-making before fabrication.

right An inspirational image is extended, almost as a doodle, and the sketches below show the transition from the original inspiration to design ideas.

below left Drawings explore the technical details of two designs. Drawing directly onto graph paper means that accuracy in terms of scale can be easily achieved, and proportions can be checked.

below right Combining different drawing materials and changing the focus helps to enliven sketches and bring different elements of the subject to the viewer's attention.

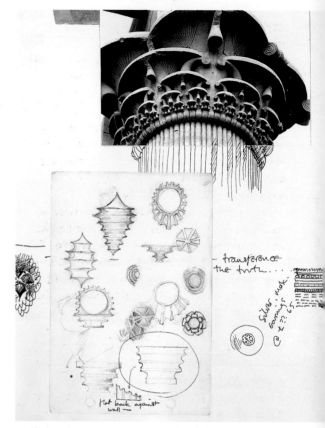

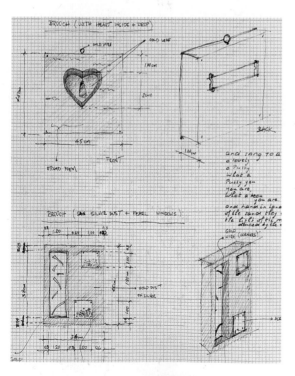

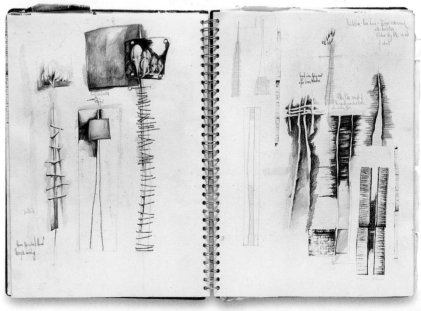

styles of drawing Just as drawing is used for a variety of purposes, so there are various types of drawing that will be utilised during the design process. You will need to establish the purpose for your drawing – what you want to communicate, and who you want to communicate it to, will dictate the style of drawing that is appropriate. Sketches, for example, are generally used to record and capture thoughts and ideas, as well as to develop them, and are therefore a crucial element of design development. (More is said about sketching on pages 30–31.)

To communicate precise in-depth information, to visually explain your intentions accurately and realise an idea, a more exact style of drawing is required. For example, if a client needs to approve a design before committing to a commission, a final rendering may be required. This is a depiction of the finished piece that is generally made prior to fabrication.

accurate drawing Technical or measured drawings are used to map out the exact dimensions and details of a piece so that a third party has an accurate account of your proposal. Technical drawing is a universal language used to relate design detailing; a piece can be drawn from every perspective so that details can be linked and examined for feasibility. Accuracy is especially important if a third party is to fabricate your designs. Mistakes can easily be made if you do not specify your requirements exactly. What seems obvious to one person is seldom so to another, and you need to ensure there is no room for error.

life drawing Because jewellery is a body-centred discipline, life drawing is considered vital for the jewellery designer. Studying the body through drawing provides essential knowledge about human proportions, movement and individual differences, all of which will be major assets for designing pieces that can be easily worn, and that will function well on the body.

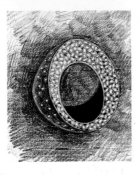

above Artistic final renderings aim to attract the eye and sell the design, and need not give the full picture from every angle.

above right Drawings can also be used to visualise compositions, displays, or placement for photography, and can be a useful record or instruction for others to work from.

centre right Accurate drawing maps out the design exactly, providing views from different angles to give a true representation of the final piece.

below and right Within the category of life drawing there are different styles. They can be almost technical, as seen in the study of the hand, or inspirational and extremely individual, as in this colourful life drawing.

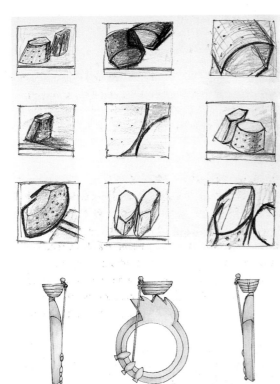

sketchbook

Recording the design process is essential. A designer's sketchbook is a diary of the design journey, in which observations and visual images are recorded, and ideas explored and developed.

practical considerations Because a sketchbook will become a valuable document, it is advisable to choose a hard-wearing, durable book that will withstand the rigours of time. A hard-backed book with good-quality paper is ideal; spiral-bound books tend to become tattered and pages are easily lost, while the pages of drawing pads can be too easily separated so that they can become lost or disordered.

The size of sketchbooks depends entirely on the individual designer; some find large expanses of paper intimidating, while others feel restricted by small pages. If you prefer to use a larger sketchbook, it might be useful to have a smaller, more portable supplementary one that you can carry around and have on hand at all times – you never know when you will want to record a significant idea or image.

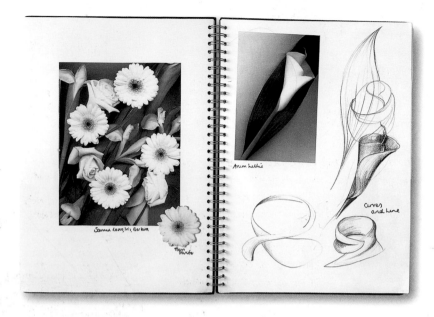

below This sketchbook is used both as a visual journal and a working tool for jotting down design possibilities. Images of food have been included, that attract the eye and arouse the senses.

above Flowers are the inspiration here, and the designer has used drawings to develop and abstract the forms, in the process creating a quite stunning sketchbook.

right Many people find doodling cathartic and relaxing. Designers who enjoy drawing and painting can take pleasure in their sketchbooks and unwind, and at the same time make beautiful visual statements.

different requirements For many people the sketchbook is both a general working journal and an amalgam of the visual and technical journal (see pages 14–17). Having separate journals is not appropriate for everyone; but in a structured learning environment, separate journals devoted to specific elements of design will help separate different areas of learning and enable a level of clarity to be maintained.

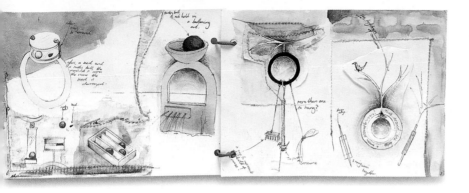

further ideas. However, a word of caution: when you first start using a sketchbook you may want to turn each page into a work of art, which could prevent you from sketching freely or enjoying the experience. Try to treat your sketchbook as a working tool that can be either utilitarian or beautiful. If you enjoy using your sketchbook it is more likely to become an artistic masterpiece than if you try too hard.

constructive and enjoyable Designers use sketchbooks to work through all aspects of design development. As you work through an idea and fill the pages of your sketchbook with images, sketches and written notes, try to highlight what is most relevant. On each page, clarify what is most important, using simple devices such emphasising lines, adding colour, ringing detail, creating windows or highlighting relevant notes. This will ensure that you can read and interpret the information clearly in later years when you might have forgotten the original stimulus or intention.

Consider too, that the more visually exciting your sketchbook is, the more it is likely to fuel and spark

above A variety of shapes, forms and devices are considered for an intriguing ring that is clearly meant to relay a message.

left Colour and form are combined with simple drawings that explore and expand on the inspiration that has been recorded in this sketchbook.

below A collage of images based on an oriental theme, pertinent to the designer's concept, allows the designer to immerse herself in visual stimulus as part of the design development process.

left By taking the time to draw a subject, a designer becomes better acquainted with the subtleties of its form. Here, a careful study of flora has captured its delicacy and beauty.

visual journal

A record of the visual world that informs a personal design language, a visual journal enables the designer to carry out and utilise visual and contextual research effectively — a tool used to develop analytical, critical, evaluative and organisational skills.

a personal language Creative designers should be constantly aware of sights, experiences and ideas that form and develop their personal design language. The visual journal is used to systematically record and collate this information. In your visual journal you should be inquisitive in a wide-ranging manner, exploring the potential of objects, subjects, situations and experiences, and trying to understand how the material you gather relates to your designs, and how it can be used to help inform future design decisions.

As you find information that stimulates your visual senses, emotions and intellect, you should be carrying out a constant process of analysis — it is vital that you understand what you feel and think about the material (see Inspiration, pages 26–29). Design is a way of harnessing your natural instinct with a cognitive process. With a raised awareness and the ability to voice your opinion about the visual world, you can begin to develop a sense of your own design philosophy.

above Layers of pages form a visual journal filled with delicate twigs and leaves that are carefully sewn into the pages, alongside drawings and colour washes.

right This visual journal is made up of accordion pleated pages so that each one can be viewed, or the whole can opened up as a single continuous sheet.

below A visual journal need not necessarily be in book form. Here numerous unlikely objects are transformed into objects of desire, collated in multiples on cards that are then suspended in their own display case.

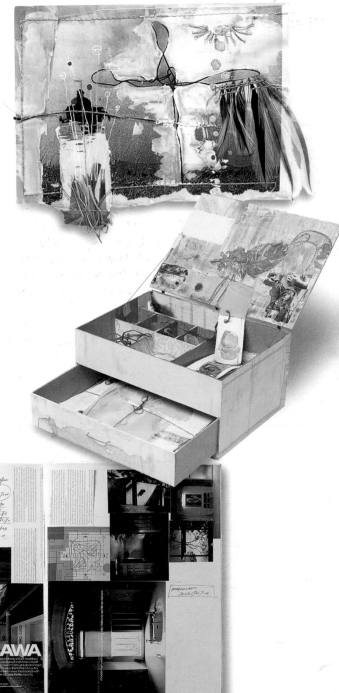

content and function

It is possible to include visual and other inspirational material in your sketchbook, but a visual journal plays a subtly different role. The material you collect in a visual journal may not as yet, or for that matter ever, be related to a specific design concept or outcome. It is a record of things that have inspired and stimulated you. It can be likened to a diary, or even a scrapbook, and should reflect in visual terms your personal responses to objects, experiences, challenges and events. The information in your visual journal should extend and expand your design thinking so that it becomes a central resource for your work.

It is essential that you establish a form for your visual journal that suits your way of thinking and working so that it is easy to maintain and access the information. It should focus on expanding and exploring all aspects of the visual and design world with particular emphasis on increasing your knowledge of form, texture, space, line, function, quality, materials, processes and so on. It might be a combination of sketches, diagrams, drawings, samples, objects, photographs, literature, philosophy – in fact anything you find stimulating.

above Cuttings, drawings and photography record valuable images for future reference.

above right Feathers are transformed from ordinary to interesting in a composition from a visual journal.

right A collection of found objects are treated with reverence and housed in a specially made box.

right An affinity with sublime and atmospheric architecture and interior design is evident in this visual journal.

technical journal

A technical journal is used specifically to record processes, explorations and outcomes of a technical nature. It helps to round off the design process and focus on the business of fabrication.

a practical reference Like a sketchbook, a technical journal is dedicated to a specific purpose, but in this case it is about learning and exploring ideas that are based on technical issues. It can be kept as part of the sketchbook, but will be more useful if the information gathered is either kept or collated separately.

How you approach your technical journal is a matter of individual choice and will also depend on the stage you are at and the way you work. For a beginner attending classes, a technical journal is useful for noting instructions along with points that you need to pay particular attention to in a way that is pertinent and personal.

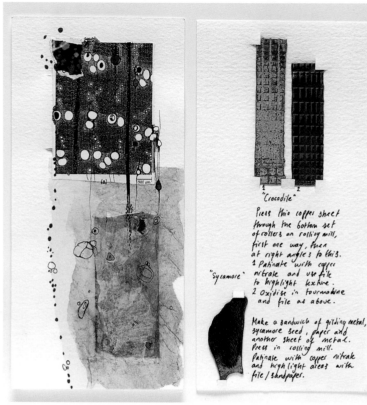

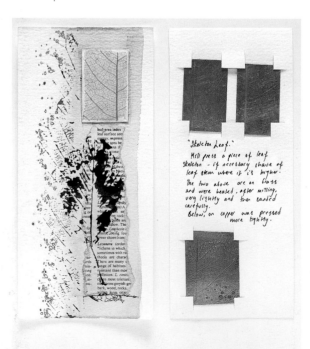

left Mill-pressed sheets of brass and copper are kept as a record, with instructions on how to re-create the different effects.

above These pages explore textural effects. On the right-hand side, copper sheets have been treated to produce a crocodile skin effect.

below The complex art of enamelling is explored and recorded. The original test pieces are then included for future reference.

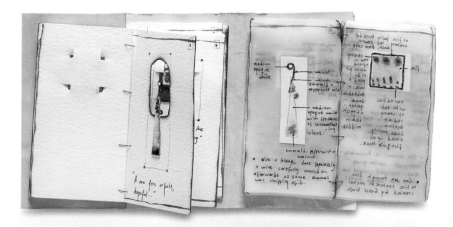

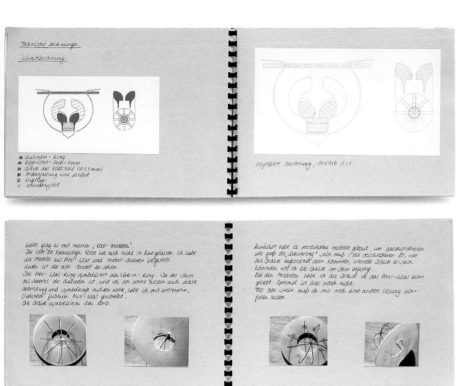

noted in order to pre-empt and prevent accidents. Often skilled craftspeople use a technical journal to record the stages of a process involving variables or a number of different factors, enabling the outcomes to be repeated or refined. The technical journal is also a good place to draw up a cutting list that includes the weight and cost of precious materials. Information such as templates and technical drawings should also be retained as part of a cohesive record.

Such journal entries are extremely valuable, as they provide information to refer back to when developing new designs in the future, and as a 'recipe' that can be used for remaking a piece. Testing or developing a design in the workshop, it is easy for the order of play to become confused or jumbled, for important stages to be left out, or for the relevance of information to be simply forgotten. A technical journal is one way of avoiding having to constantly reinvent the wheel.

When learning a new skill you may find that your notes act as a better prompt than a textbook, as they will be self-tailored to your needs. As you encounter problems, record them in your journal together with the solution so you can avoid making the same mistake again in a similar scenario.

Keeping a technical journal is not difficult if you view it as an extension of your tool kit; whenever you are at the bench or in the workshop it should be on hand to record the process. Jewellery making and design is a complex business, it is important that technical factors be considered and developed as part of the design process so that you can plan fabrication.

a recipe book Before fabrication you may need to plan technical requirements, so the journal might include a record of sourcing a specialist material, with appropriate technical information, samples, trials and outcomes. Health and safety information should also be

above The fabrication of a piece is recorded with technical drawings and photographs as well as detailed text.

right Prior to fabrication, the form is mapped out in a technical journal to check details and proportions before a template is made.

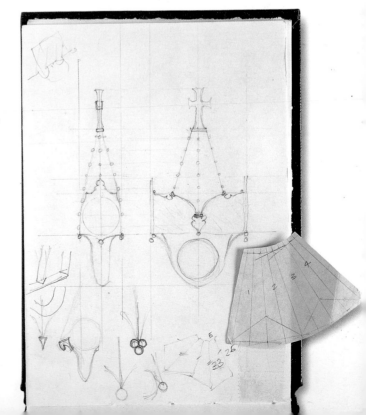

craft skills

Craft skill is the practical expertise, gained through specialist training, that is used for construction of samples, test pieces and during final fabrication.

essential knowledge Strictly speaking, craft skills are not absolutely necessary for designing jewellery, but a sound knowledge of processes, materials and jewellery-related skills does facilitate the designer's prediction of a design's outcomes with some level of accuracy, and is extremely useful throughout the design development process.

Even though a designer may not actually make the final piece, it will aid the design process if they are able to make samples, test pieces, technical trials, models and prototypes. Being an expert practitioner is not a necessity. Indeed there are so many different branches of jewellery fabrication that it would be virtually impossible to have a truly comprehensive portfolio of practical skills without spending considerable time immersed in learning and practising. However, a good

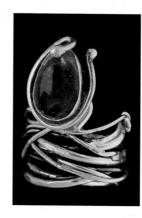

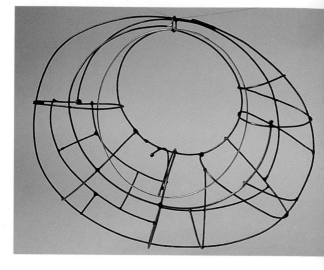

left Traditional craft skills, such as stone setting, are used to make this striking silver ring.

above Before fabrication, a maquette can be made using basic craft skills, which will inform the designer about form, scale, and aesthetics.

below Various craft skills have been used in making silver samples that explore individual effects using traditional techniques.

grounding is vitally important, as it provides a valuable understanding of the characteristics and limitations of materials and processes or techniques that might be used in your designs.

There are a few key skills and techniques, such as piercing, filing, forming, soldering and polishing, which are not too difficult to learn and develop and which will significantly increase a designer's ability to make simple models or casting masters. These skills can be self-taught with a limited number of appropriate tools, a small space in the home and good technical books. There are also many evening classes, summer schools or short courses that teach basic jewellery-making skills.

individual style Having craft skills gives you an advantage throughout the many stages of design, but they can also be a means of establishing your own style. To create a recognisable and personal identity as a designer, it is important that people can distinguish your designs from those of others, and the ability to fabricate

your own designs can make the difference between the ordinary and the unique – for example, you are more likely to be in a position to develop new ways of applying established skills in an individual and innovative manner. Many jewellery designers create their own design style via a technique taken in a personal direction, and have established careers based on designs using particular skills and techniques.

specialist skills There is a common misconception that a single jeweller is totally responsible for the fabrication of a piece, but this is unlikely. Often, in specialist areas such as stone setting or enamelling for example, skilled craftspeople will be employed to ensure and maintain the highest standards of fabrication.

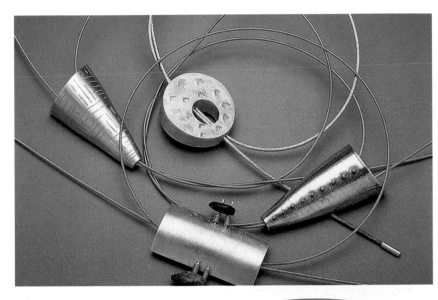

above An understanding of a variety of craft skills would be useful in order to design, not to mention fabricate, these delightful multimedia neckpieces.

right Competent craft skills are essential for making earrings such as these. Made of 18-ct gold, any mistakes would be costly.

left Traditional jewellery skills and techniques, such as filing and carring, are applied to make acrylic samples as trials of form, textures and colour.

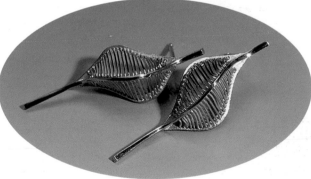

Even if you are a skilled craftsperson, it is unlikely that you will be sufficiently proficient across the board to be able to fabricate all of your own designs yourself, and you will probably have to rely on others for the execution of specialist skills such as stone setting, casting, enamelling, spinning or engraving, to name but a few. When relying on others, it is important to establish a good relationship; a sensitive and able craftsperson who can interpret your designs accurately may become indispensable to you, but remember the sentiment might not be mutual! (See Fabrication, pages 44–45.)

CHAPTER TWO
STAGES OF THE DESIGN PROCESS

Designing well takes time, effort, and a little aptitude. Rather like driving a car, the theory sounds simple enough, but there is more to the process than meets the eye. It takes time and practice to master the various actions required and to connect the various stages – finding inspiration, defining the concept, brainstorming, sketching, researching, model making, etc. Without the ability to perform and connect these stages efficiently and effectively, decisions and connections may be tenuous or inappropriate, and designs may be imbalanced.

As with so many things that we do, the more you practise these stages, both as individual actions and in the context of the whole design process, the better at them you will become. As your designs become more successful and sophisticated your confidence will grow, as will your enthusiasm.

design development

Understanding what constitutes design development is fundamental to successful design. Without the ability to develop a design, the conclusions reached are usually rudimentary and based on instinct alone rather than on well-informed decisions.

identifying questions Design development is about understanding problems and finding solutions, then honing these solutions so that they are cohesive, relevant and appropriate.

To develop a design you need first to identify the questions that need to be answered. For instance, 'what shape do I want my design to be?' To answer that question you need to consider the relevance of shape for your concept. If you want to design a piece that is to appear aggressive, for example, a triangle would, at face value, seem to be more appropriate than a circle. However, you may specifically want to use a circle, in which case you would need to explore the possibilities of a circular shape in more detail. Can a circle be aggressive, and if so, how? You might perhaps decide that a handcuff or stocks could suit your concept, but this in turn might create further questions, such as 'are there any other forms of restraint that are circular in form?'

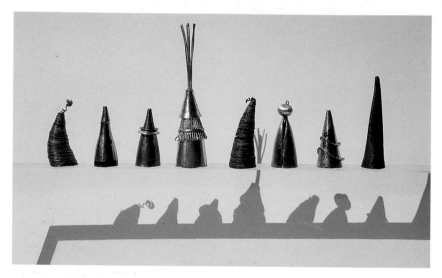

below left Different possibilities are explored for this heavily concept-based design so that the solutions proposed are appropriate, and the design is cohesive.

above Samples are made as part of the design development process so that shape, form, colour, texture, materials and processes can be tested.

below right A number of bizarre ideas for a ring form are explored in drawings that clearly illustrate lateral thinking and an enjoyment of the design process.

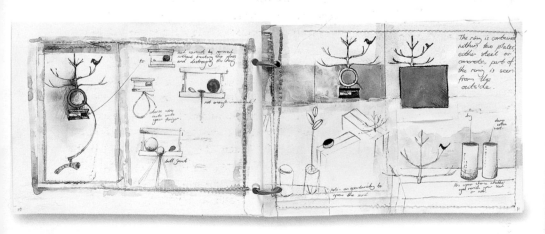

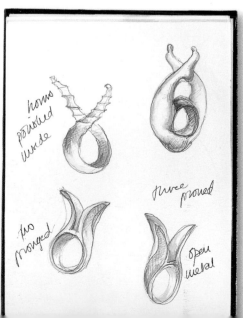

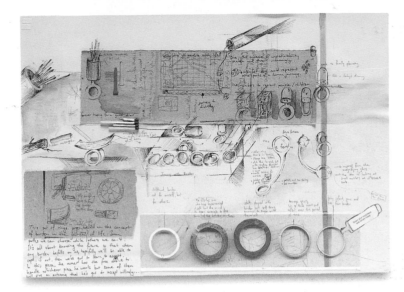

By considering relevant questions your decision becomes an informed one and will be more appropriate to the concept.

Often when one asks the question 'why,' an answer comes back that is nonspecific and noncommittal. For example, if asked why you chose a certain colour you might reply that you like it, but if you were then asked to explain why you like it you would have to consider the reason. If you take time to think about your choices and examine your motives, you will be in a better position to make conscious and informed decisions.

above In-depth sketches, notes, and samples are made to find the most appropriate symbols and forms for a series of rings.

above right A variety of positive and negative shapes are explored for designs to be made of metal and leather. Drawn on graph paper, the scale and the pattern can be considered together.

left The familiar cross form has been altered and developed in these sketches. The designer has used watercolour paints so that the design may be more easily visualised in the proposed materials.

thinking laterally

Lateral thinking involves looking at something and seeing beyond the obvious. The opposite of literal thinking, it is about finding original and exciting solutions through indirect methods, while still maintaining a clear link to the subject. The process of design development is heavily reliant on lateral thinking, but for many of us this does not come naturally. Literal thinking is often the reason why the design process cannot get started, or why it stops as soon as it has begun. With practice, both can be improved over time to become increasingly more fluid.

When we consider a concept it is all too easy to see the obvious or the literal. For example, if presented with the theme of the fish, images of tropical fish with fabulous colours may spring to mind. A fish-shaped design would clearly be a literal translation, and in all likelihood, not particularly interesting. A more lateral approach might see the iridescence and translucence of the fish explored by framing specific parts of a fish (not necessarily identifiable as such), resulting in a series of enamelled brooches; the result is likely to be considerably more exciting and intriguing.

considering the elements To help organise the design process from the start, begin by listing each main 'element' to be considered during design development. The essential elements of design (see the design checklist, opposite page) include shape, form, texture, colour, the five senses, emotion, function, materials and processes, and together will constitute your design intention. Look at what is required of each element, work through each systematically, and consider how you intend to make the individual elements mesh and work together. Of course some elements may be more pertinent to your concept than others, but by considering them all, at least to some degree, you can be confident of not overlooking something that may contribute greatly to the development process, and, ultimately, to the final design.

below A variety of materials is considered as part of the design process so that the concept can be further accentuated by the appropriate material.

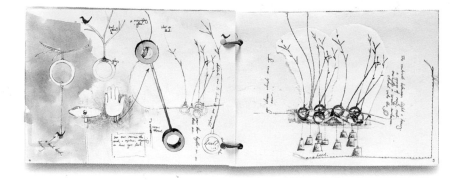

above Simple sketches are accompanied by the designer's notes in a sketchbook that acts as a blackboard and a record for thoughts and comments.

applying design development Design development can seem daunting if you try to address everything at once. Take an individual aspect of your idea, identify the inherent qualities, then develop, hone, and refine the idea to make best use of the quality. On reaching a fitting conclusion, consider another element in conjunction with the last, and further develop the

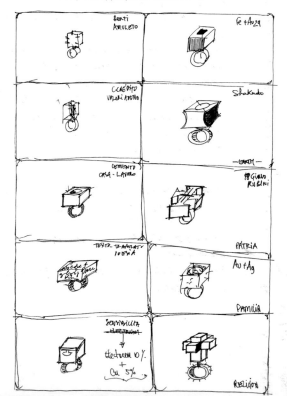

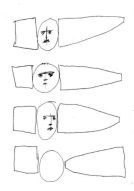

above Subtle changes of shape and configuration are explored in these quick sketches.

right More detailed drawings of a brooch facilitate decisions about materials and process.

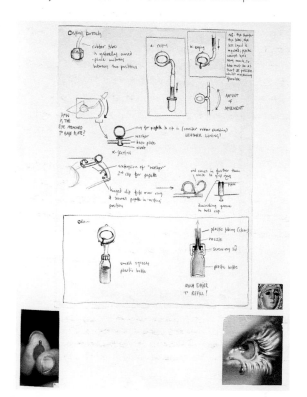

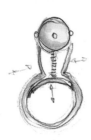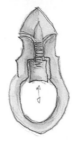

above Quick sketches of rings are a means of noting an idea prompted by a preoccupation with changing size; the sketches may not immediately be developed further, but they are material for future reference.

design. Keep building on your conclusions, repeating the process until you have considered every element and aspect of the design.

In developing a design you will have explored new ideas and discovered different directions for finding suitable material to work with. Once you have identified a number of alternatives, you will need to review the material to judge how relevant it is to your concept, and how it stands up to the criteria established in the design brief. Not all of your material will be appropriate. Decide what is relevant, and retain only what is useful for your design. But don't forget to store away alternate ideas for future reference.

A design development process should resemble a voyage of discovery. There will be certain points at which you should pause to record, or 'map' images of particular interest, and there will also be points where ideas are provoked – these too should be noted down as though you were keeping a diary.

The important fact to remember about your voyage is that you are not a passenger, you are the driver and explorer – it is you who establishes the purpose of the journey and dictates the route. Just as no two people or projects will be exactly the same, so there can be no definitive path for everyone to follow.

centre and right An inspirational image is stored in a sketchbook for reference because it prompted a series of designs in which the essence of the form was abstracted and then combined with the design intention – size alteration of rings.

design checklist

The factors on this checklist are essential elements that should be considered during design development. According to the concept behind a particular design, some may be more important than others, but if any are ignored, the design may not reach its full potential. Each point on the checklist needs to be cross-referenced to the design brief and the concept.

- **shape** Is the shape of the piece appropriate for the brief? Is the scale of the piece appropriate for good aesthetic and visual balance?
- **form** Have you considered the piece from all angles? Is the piece too flat/two-dimensional?
- **texture** What finish should the piece have?
- **colour** Does the piece need colour? What does the colour need to achieve?
- **the 5 senses** How will they be engaged?
- **emotion** What emotional impact do you want the piece to make?
- **function** Will the piece be able to perform the function that is required of it?
- **materials** What materials are suitable for the design? Will the chosen materials have the appropriate properties for the job?
- **process** Is it possible to make the design? What processes are appropriate for fabricating the piece? Do you intend the process itself to help define the piece or complement the design intention?

✳

Two very practical questions that might define the parameters of design development are:

- **schedule** How long do you have to complete the project?
- **budget** How much can you afford to spend on the project?

inspiration

Inspiration can come from an object, emotion, person, place or form, or even a process, technique or smell — it could be anything. There are no rules, and where you seek it depends on your interests. Inspiration is simply that which stimulates a reaction, anything that drives and motivates.

discovering and understanding

inspiration
Often we are unaware of what really inspires us, as we tend to take a great deal for granted. We are inclined to react subconsciously to something we see or feel without really focusing on it, let alone taking the time to analyse the initial reaction. Getting to know what really inspires you as an individual involves being able to stand back from a subject and look at it both subjectively and objectively at the same time. You need to learn to think about what you are confronting and then ask yourself exactly what it makes you feel, and why.

For designers, inspiration is only the beginning. The next step is to understand the nature of the inspiration; if you don't know why a thing inspires you, it cannot be used consciously and constructively in design terms. Each subject presents a wealth of possibilities and an

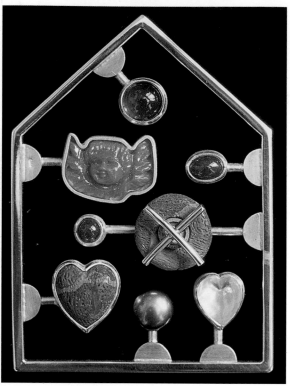

above and left Photographs (left) act as inspiration for a designer who sees beauty in the most unlikely subjects; these images then act as the inspiration for a brooch where elements of the inspiration are abstracted and transformed through the design process.

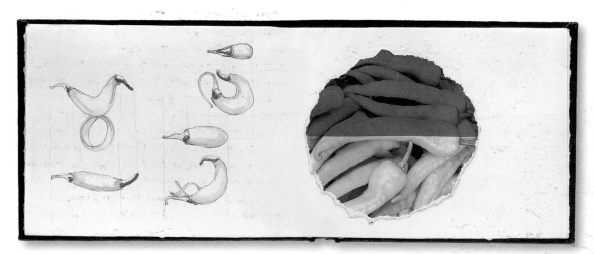

left The notion of chillies being too hot to handle is used as inspiration for pieces where the wearer is protected from the chillies' potential heat

above left The bold silver forms of these rings utilise and complement the form, colour and texture of the inspirational foodstuffs.

above right The colours and textures of these assorted exotic dried foodstuffs are inspiration for a collection of rings.

below In these striking silver rings the structure of a sea urchin can still be easily seen as the inspiration for the design.

infinite number of ways to view it – the important thing is to identify the 'language' of your inspiration and the way in which it is universally understood so that you can use that information intelligently.

With a greater understanding of inspiration, designs can gain a clear and confident voice, and more accurately express intentions. Without this understanding, the development process and finished designs can be rather bland and uneventful, and will almost certainly lack genuine character or individuality.

identifying the parts To start to form a design based on your inspiration, it helps to examine the constituent parts so that you are familiar with each and every component. You will then need to consider how many of these components are essential and how many are not; how many elements can be removed from the equation before the inspiration becomes simply ordinary. For example take a bird or chicken – not the most obvious form of inspiration for jewellery perhaps, but nonetheless filled with possibility. Consider its shape in profile as a two-dimensional image, its form as a three-dimensional object, its internal skeleton or structure, skin texture, feather colour, the movement of the creature, joint articulation or physical and aesthetic

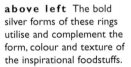

balance. Depending on your intentions, the profile of the bird alone may be all that is necessary to relay your concept, but if you need to show the beauty of a bird then perhaps colour, texture and an accurate form would also be required. There is a great deal that is inspiring in the most unlikely objects if you just know how to look.

considering the effect By abstracting the information we can decide what really attracts us to a subject. One aspect of the inspiration might be its ability to give a feeling of comfort – for example, evoking calm, ease, and perhaps complacency. A design could be given a tactile quality, like a weather-worn pebble, that invites one to handle and caress it, thereby creating a calming effect.

right The effect that inspiration has on the subconscious can be used to advantage, as can be seen in forms inspired by razor blades, which evoke a sense of discomfort.

below A collection of inspirational images is collated so that the connection between them is obvious – this grouping also enriches the individual images resulting in a more impacting display.

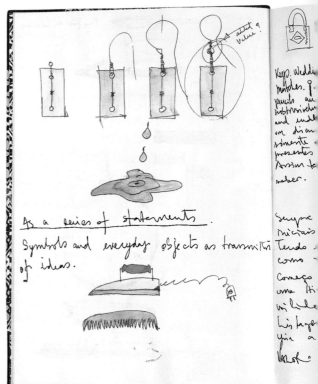

Surprisingly, however, what inspires us or draws us to something may well be that which makes us feel uncomfortable. Our state of awareness is heightened when we are consciously or subconsciously put on our guard. If we understand why certain things cause us comfort or discomfort, we can use this information consciously in the design process. A piece that exploits subject matter that is generally considered unpleasant is likely to attract attention because most people have a morbid desire to be shocked.

individual and universal appeal Once you have these answers, you can begin to consider how to translate the properties of the inspiration into a design in an evocative way so that it provokes similar reactions in others. In some cases this is relatively simple. People tend to share many criteria of beauty, as well as having certain experiences, prejudices, interests and viewpoints in common. There are many things, such as a beautiful shell, a flower or a sublime landscape, that have universal appeal. The inspiration for a piece can sometimes seem predictable, however, each designer's response to a subject will be different, as will be the way in which it is handled and interpreted. Love, for example, is an inspiration almost as old as time itself. Every angle and permutation has been explored in literature, in plays and films, in art and in jewellery, yet it is a theme that will always endure, continuing to inspire unique work that speaks a universal language.

However, on occasions the source of a jeweller's inspiration may be quite unexpected and not at all obvious to others. This presents the designer with another challenge; to pass on their own inspiration to a wider audience by emulating its characteristics in their designs. The secret lies in being able to abstract its essence, the thing or things, the quality, that defines the inspiration.

right A process can also act as inspiration, as it produces a desire to create objects of beauty. These highly individual samples of cut stone will in turn be the inspiration for jewellery.

below left Inspirational objects collected from a walk in the countryside have been thoughtfully displayed in a visual journal to be used in future designs.

below right "Pop out parts" from self assembly toy kits are recorded in a quick sketch as inspiration for a future brooch design.

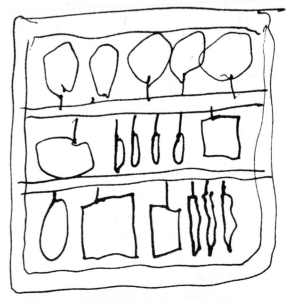

sketching

Sketching is the shorthand of drawing. Sketches can be quick drawings used to note and outline an idea, or studies of a more finished piece of work.

visual ideas Artists and designers are visual people who see ideas as images rather than words, so it is essential to be able to put these down before they are forgotten or overridden by other more mundane preoccupations. If you see something that stimulates you, or perhaps chance upon an outstanding solution to a vexing problem, being able to note it down as a quick sketch will enable you to recall it with greater clarity at a later date.

Sketching is used both before and throughout the design process to explore and record images and ideas. Just as a writer may make quick notes of phrases or snatches of overheard conversation, a designer should be ready to note down an image. This should ideally be an ongoing process. It is often difficult to hold the thread of a long conversation, and, in the same way, it is hard to keep track of the numerous images that fly

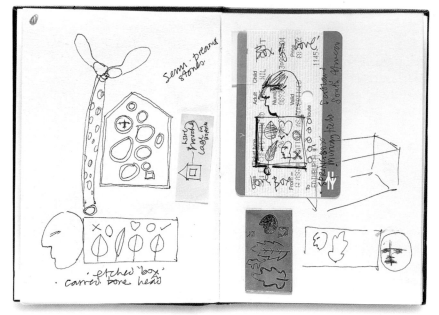

below left This atmospheric sketch is made up of layers of photocopied images, silhouettes and lettering as well as pencil line, colour and stitchwork.

above A designer may have to make use of whatever is available to quickly record an idea, and collate it in the sketchbook later; here a train ticket has been used.

below Different features of a bird are examined in detailed sketches that focus on colour, structure, pattern and form.

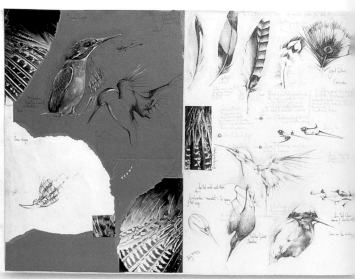

left An extravagant colour sketch is used to create a fabulous abstract composition that invites the viewer to consider a personal interpretation of the subject.

might be the texture that interests you, or possibly the mechanics. The area of your focus will dictate how much of the image needs to be detailed. For example, to indicate context or form, a simple outline might be all that is required.

form a habit Like many things in life, sketching becomes easier the more you do it. Initially your sketches may appear crude to you, but with practice you will gain confidence and purpose, and the sketches will be less self-conscious and more useful. Try not to be overly concerned with making a pretty drawing, as this might cause you to expend too much energy on looks. Accurate description should be the main concern.

Try using different drawing materials to enliven your sketches and widen your range, so that you can focus on and define detail. Using a pen or pencil alone is fine, but the addition of colour and visual texture not only provides relief to the eye but may also help you to explore your ideas in more depth. In addition, it can lift a sketch so that it becomes less ordinary and more likely to stimulate further ideas.

around in our minds as a train of thought progresses. Sketches keep track of images and ideas in much the same way that minutes record a meeting.

Making a visual record of the progression of an idea enables you to return to a particular image or idea to develop it further. It also helps to keep your mind focused and uncluttered so that you don't waste energy trying to memorise information.

defining the intention Unlike artists' sketches, those made by designers are not simply concerned with composition, tonal balance and so on. There are any number of things you might want to record or explore, and to do so quickly and efficiently, it is necessary to decide what exactly it is that you want to achieve. It

above Even quick sketches can be highly individual and informative; this faithful hound is clearly on a mission.

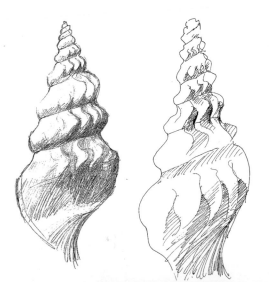

left Two sketches of a shell focus on different aspects of the form, resulting in sketches that convey specific information such as surface detail and tonal contrast.

right The beauty of a city skyline is captured in a sketch that suggests the exotic character and flavour of the culture and its inhabitants.

design brief

The design brief is an essential first step towards designing a piece of jewellery, as it is the statement of intent that helps to define the expectations of the piece.

aspects of a design brief A brief can include any number of aspects that may be considered during the design process from concept, context, cost, materials, scale, production processes, time frame and end user to scale of the piece, size of a collection, and when, where and how it is to be presented.

Good design is generally the result of a focused cognitive process. Before you begin designing you should take time to consider and define a design brief that considers the various aspects of design relevant to that project. This will help to direct your design development and make the design process more productive.

writing a design brief Not every project will have a formal design brief, but it is worthwhile to take the time to write one. A brief is indispensable as it is the means by which you can outline the parameters of a project so that the results can be predicted to a greater extent. When writing a design brief it is important that specific goals should be identified clearly so there is little room for confusion.

the value of diamonds

Consider the value of diamonds and design a fine jewellery piece that reflects your view on the value of diamonds

The piece should be made from precious materials and should contain no fewer than three diamonds that can be any size, shape or colour

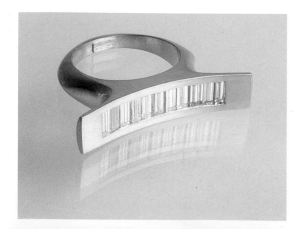

above right Entitled 'The Key to Chastity', this ring-cum-pendant makes a wry comment on the engagement ring. A diamond is set at the shaft of the key, and two more are set in either end of the T-bar clasp.

left This 18-ct white gold ring with channel-set baguette diamonds is titled 'We worship at the altar of Mammon', clearly a comment on wealth as a false but alluring god.

Even if you are given a brief it is advisable that you also write a personal design brief, as this will help to clarify your own personal intentions. It is a device used to express your aims and objectives, and will give your project a sense of purpose and direction. A personal design brief is a tool that makes it easier for you to concentrate your thoughts so that they can be kept relevant, it is all too easy to become sidetracked and distracted by good ideas that are not relevant to the project at hand.

styles of design brief Briefs are likely to differ considerably according to the context in which they are written or presented. For example, a competition brief may be used to convey a challenge of some sort, while a brief set in an educational context would logically be used to introduce or highlight one or more aspects of a particular learning experience.

The presentation and contents of briefs differ greatly. There is no set format for how they should be written or presented, so they can look surprisingly dissimilar. A brief that is obscurely worded can be immensely difficult to interpret, while a thorough brief can seem overly restrictive and leave little room for imagination. Whatever the style, take time to absorb and assimilate the information contained in the brief, as often it is just the presentation and order of the brief that are off-putting.

interpreting the brief There is no easy solution to interpreting a design brief, and the important thing is to take time to consider and identify what is really relevant so that you can focus the design process. However clear or obscure a brief is, it will generally be a skeleton onto which you need to put some flesh. Concentrate on the key points in the original brief and keep referring to these so that you do not lose sight of the objectives of the project.

relationships

Design a two-piece set of jewellery where the emphasis of the design is about the relationship between the two pieces

✳

Think about the set as having complementary characteristics such as principle, philosophy, puzzle, union, concept or harmony, as with yin and yang

above and left The traditional stones that one would expect to find in these two rings have been cleverly replaced with candles. The relationship is clearly their function – perhaps they would be given to mark a celebration such as a birthday.

below A neckpiece and brooch are already linked by the delicacy of their forms, but also have a more obvious physical relationship. The wearer can decide how the pieces are positioned, and the open conical brooch acts as a cap for one end of the knitted silver neckpiece.

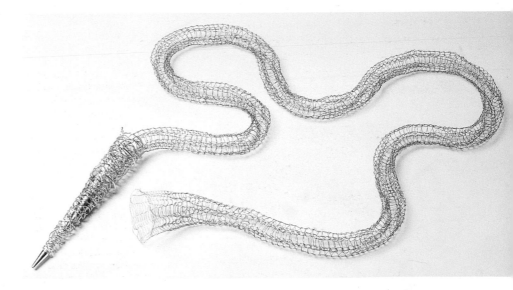

concept

A concept is the idea behind a design, the intention of the piece. It is what you intend to say to your audience through your work, which is your statement of intent.

the need for a concept The notion of a concept is sometimes viewed with scepticism and seen as an unnecessary element, but in fact it is of paramount importance. Design begins with inspiration, but without a well-defined concept and a firm idea about how to translate or use the inspiration, the design process will tend to be more accidental than intentional, imparting a similarly accidental character to the final design. That is not to say that a piece made without a deliberate concept will fail, but a little thought and analysis will identify a concept behind the vast majority of good pieces of design.

right There is a clear conceptual intention to relay geographical information in this series of design development sketches for a brooch to commemorate Christmas.

below left and right These two pendants are based on the concept of emotional frailty. In one, the concept is communicated through the egg in its centre, which represents the fragile human ego and potential growth. The other pendant reaches a more optimistic conclusion; with the self-assurance that comes with maturity, the fledgling is ready to leave behind the naivete of youth.

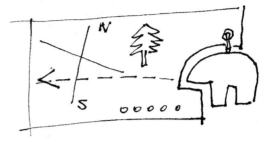

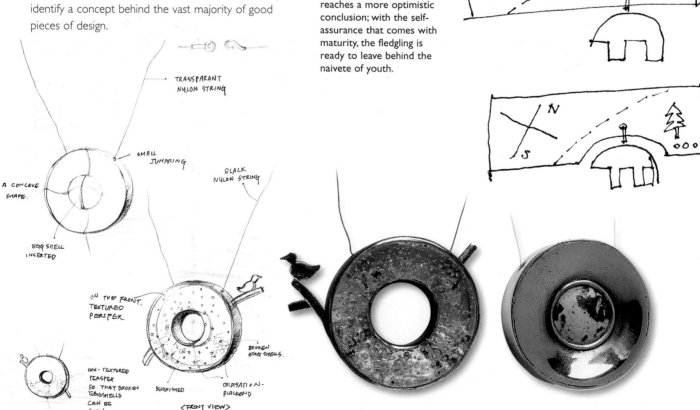

TRANSPARANT NYLON STRING

SMALL JUMPRING

A CONCAVE SHAPE.

BLACK NYLON STRING

EGG SHELL INSERTED

ON THE FRONT. TEXTURED PERSPEX.

BROKEN EGG SHELLS.

NON-TEXTURED PERSPEX SO THAT BROKEN EGGSHELLS CAN BE SEEN.

BURNISHED

OXIDISATION- BLACKEND

〈BACK VIEW〉

〈FRONT VIEW〉

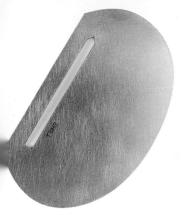

left The wearer of this piece is invited to interact with the pendant form; the arrow in the slit hints at a direction and a base, but the piece dictates that the wearer be the decision-maker.

Defining the concept clearly at the start allows the design process to be decisive and well focused, so that you are able to find the most relevant solutions and reach more exact and exciting conclusions. A selection of creative concepts is explored in Chapter 4 (pages 96–155).

keeping it simple A simple concept is often considerably more successful than a complex one, as it is less likely to tax the imagination or intellect of your audience. A concept can easily be over-worked and become so convoluted that it is unintelligible to all but the designer. A concept that is not well carried through may be the result of relying too much on tenuous connections rather than concentrating on the central idea. Similarly, if a design concept is so exclusive that it can only reach an audience of one, it is highly probable that the work will not have the appeal that the designer wants or intends.

In such cases it would be advisable to rethink the design and content with a view to making it more intelligible, which may involve simplifying and clarifying the concept. It is important to retain the main focus throughout and not to clutter your ideas with non-essential peripheral information. A good test is to try to clearly articulate your concept. If you find you cannot explain it well verbally, the chances are that others will not understand your intentions, in which case further refinement is necessary.

above This piece expresses an emotional state – if you are feeling too emotionally fragile the piece can be worn as a warning to those who may otherwise be heavy handed.

right Titled 'Eternal Life', the unbroken form relays a sense of continuity, while the carefully crafted natural materials refer to the endless cycle of life.

below The idea of something being too hot to handle is explored with images of a chilli that has been wrapped for our protection; in some of the designs wording is used as a decorative device that also compounds the concept.

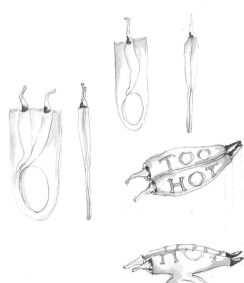

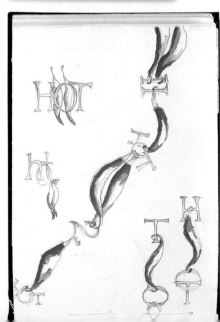

brainstorming

Brainstorming is about considering every option – thrashing out an idea so that every possibility is considered and the design process can reach its full potential.

opening up the mind To ensure that your designs are not based only on the most simplistic ideas, you need to first consider what is obvious about your concept and then look beyond the initial ideas to find solutions that are more interesting, sophisticated or subtle.

First impressions of a subject are usually based on purely instinctive reactions, but after this you need to scrutinise your inspiration and concept, and inquire further. Brainstorming is a process of opening up the mind to all the possibilities by intensive exploration and

right A variety of interpretations of a simple circular form are noted so that the designer can focus on the different associations with the form as part of the design process.

below left Ideas concerning the needs and desires of a person who may want a personal pill container that can also be worn as a piece of jewellery are brainstormed to identify what some of the requirements of the piece and the wearer might be.

below right A variety of icons for wealth is brainstormed before a shortlist is made and a design is developed based on the concept of opulence.

examination – it is about looking for connections that are perhaps more obscure, exciting, challenging, provocative or amusing.

By allowing ideas to flow without restriction and recording them on paper as they occur, you can begin to move away from simple ideas into new directions, exploring areas of interest that might not have occurred to you at the outset. If possible, discuss your ideas with

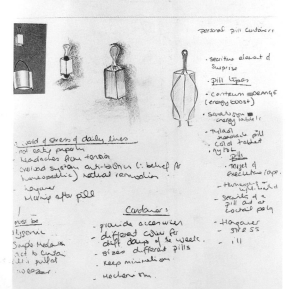

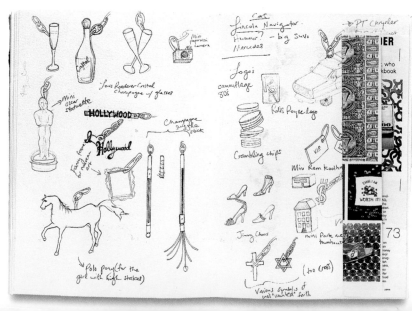

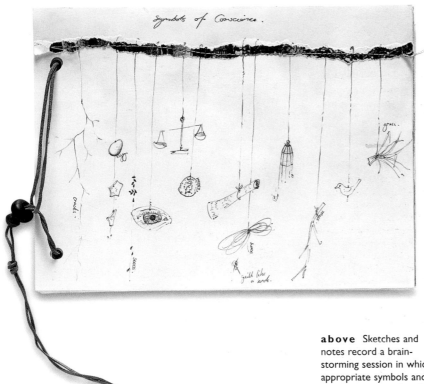

Symbols of Conscience.

with the initial subject or idea in the centre, and subsequent related ideas linked by a 'web' travelling outwards. Similarly, the family-tree graph places the focal idea at the 'root' with the different trains of thought branching up and out.

sifting the information
Ideas can flow fast in a brainstorming session, so you may quickly find that you have a great deal of information that requires sifting. You will need to be discerning to identify the ideas that have the most potential. Shortlist the best ideas by highlighting them, and then decide which have the most relevance for your design brief before you take them further through research and development. Try to identify whether any ideas overlap, and if so where, as this is valuable information that can be used to strengthen your concept.

Don't be afraid of extremes, as these can lead to new and invigorating ways of thinking, and, of course, they can always be tempered to make them appear less radical.

above Sketches and notes record a brainstorming session in which appropriate symbols and wording were explored for a conceptual piece based on the burden of conscience.

other people, as they will often have a different perspective from yours, which may provide valuable insights.

organising the process
Start by writing down the idea that you want to explore; this will be the focal point for your brainstorming session. One idea will readily act as a catalyst for further ones if you can free your mind and thoughts. Expand your concept one level at a time, writing down your initial responses as subdivisions of the original idea. These subdivisions should then prompt more ideas and hence further subdivisions.

How you record this process is important, as you will need to be able to access the information easily. One way to do this is with a spider graph, which starts

right A spider graph shows the train of thought and new ideas that arose during a brainstorming session on the subject of religion.

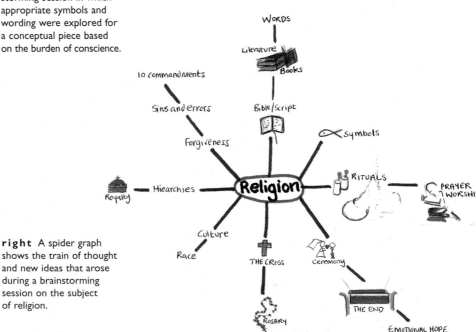

research

Research is the process of systematic investigation with the purpose of increasing knowledge and finding new or better solutions, a means of broadening your outlook and enriching your designs.

broadening your horizons When you have found something inspiring, you need to gain as much information and knowledge about it as possible.

If, for example, your object of interest is a fish – you might find it beautiful, stimulating, or even repugnant – and you want to form a design around the subject or the feelings it inspires, it might be beneficial to actually handle a fish, to feel its texture and weight, to know in detail how it looks, feels, smells and tastes. If, specifically, the look or feel of a fish interests you, more academic research would explain exactly how the scales of a fish protect, move and reflect light. Research of a more general nature might reveal important elements that could affect the interpretation of a design, such as surrounding symbolism. In this case, a fish is commonly recognised as a symbol of Christianity. It is this kind of information that can become the catalyst for ideas and unexpected design directions.

right Magazine clippings that include an image of a stealth bomber are collated in a sketchbook to research striking forms seen in manmade objects and architecture.

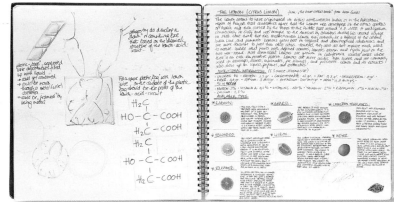

left and above Lemons are researched in depth so that everything that can be gleaned about the lemon as a subject is explored – from type and chemical composition to tools for squeezing – in order to broaden the designer's knowledge of the subject.

Some of the required knowledge you may already have stored in your head. However, people often tend to consider things at a superficial level and it may be necessary to refresh your memory through research to recover information stored in your subconscious.

research material There are so many sources of research material that it would be quite impossible to identify them all. Consider where the information you need is most likely to be found. For example, if you wanted to research the Art Deco movement, a library would be the obvious place to start, but if you were looking for innovative methods of containment it might be more fruitful to examine containers and products found on the high street. The internet has become a useful resource, and search engines can reveal less obvious sources of information.

above left Shells and other natural objects were collected, photographed and stored in a visual journal, alongside sketches that further research natural forms.

below left Notes and images based around Japanese architecture are researched and collated alongside images of samples and models of the final bangle designs.

above Various images of flowers are researched that will be used as inspiration for the form of a ring.

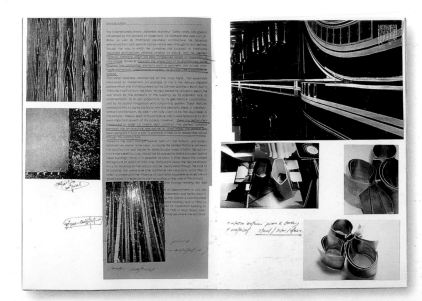

filtering the research When your research is design-specific, it will be necessary at some point to filter the material, and you will need to return to the original concept and the design brief to check that you have not strayed too far from either one.

Research need not be exclusively led by a narrow design question. It may be an ongoing process of gathering information that informs a particular body of work. It is important to be open to new ideas and directions during the research process, and to retain and collate information so it can be referred to as part of your overall portfolio. Try to be discerning about how you use your research, but keep any good material that proves unsuitable for one project, as it could be the inspiration or information needed for future work.

samples & test pieces

Samples and test pieces are specimens or small portions of the total piece intended to show its character and quality, and test standards.

information and clarification If you have a material in mind for the fabrication of a piece, it is advisable to take time to locate the material and collect samples so you can check its quality and its suitability for the purpose. If you want to explore different ways of treating that material, perhaps to create a different look or texture, or even to alter its properties, you will need to conduct a series of tests.

Samples and test pieces are physical pieces used as part of an information-gathering and clarification process. They present another valuable opportunity to ensure that you are making appropriate decisions.

Samples are usually concerned with detail and concentrate on small segments of a larger scheme. For example, you might make samples of a commercially manufactured material such as latex because you are concerned about the suitability of

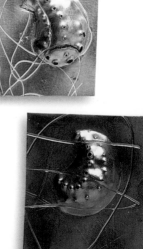

above A collection of vibrant samples is used to help with decisions both for design development and for fabrication.

left A deluge of paper samples is used to test different combinations of colour and shape, and to create inspirational textures and forms.

right Test pieces explore a variety of materials and textures that could be used to express the delicate texture and form of a spider's body.

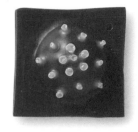

left Various test pieces and samples are kept as part of the process of understanding materials, forms, textures and processes to enlighten, broaden and inform design development.

below Acrylic test pieces test combinations of colour, texture and process so that these outcomes can be assessed and brought to bear on the design process.

0.533mm (0.021 inches) of latex in comparison with 0.813mm (0.032 inches). You would want to have samples of these materials for trials as well as for future reference.

Samples can be a limited example or a 'taster' of a technique, in much the same way as a knitting or fabric swatch shows a small segment of the whole. If you find you are interested in a particular process, samples are a way of exploring and progressing it.

inspiration and posterity As well as a means of answering technical and aesthetic questions, samples are a useful source of inspiration because they are about choice; samples and test pieces are precious tangible illustrations, often the first windows into what can actually be, rather than ideas in your head or designs on paper. They can be lovely and desirable objects in themselves, as they are usually relatively simple and pure statements – uncluttered and informal.

Collectively, they also have the potential to form a catalogue of materials, processes, textures, colours and so on. So always keep the pieces and treat them with care. They should be collated with notes that record why, how and when they were made and what they relate to. A technical journal is a logical place to record this material, but if samples are swatches of fabric or materials that relate directly to a design and are part of the decision-making process, it might be more appropriate to keep them in your sketchbook.

above Silver and copper are used with traditional oriental lacquer techniques to explore different combinations of colour and pattern.

right With a focus on a loose layered effect, paper has been treated, shaped and formed before being assembled as a sample that will inform the final design.

model making

A model is a three-dimensional representation of an intended object, generally made of lesser materials or reduced in size where appropriate. The purpose of model making is to test out ideas in three-dimensional form in order to further develop and hone a design.

testing theories Model making is often overlooked as a stage of design development, yet is an important part of the design process. In many cases, drawing cannot fully communicate the three-dimensional quality, whereas a model can provide enough information for the form to be realised in detail.

When designing, there is a tendency to avoid the detail we find awkward. The value of model making lies in its ability to confirm whether your design decisions are feasible or not. If the model does present problems, examine it carefully against the criteria laid down in your design brief in order to correct them.

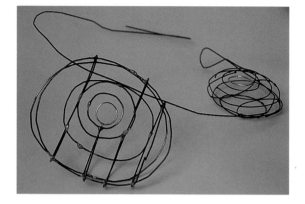

left Linear models made from binding wire, silver and gold sketch out how the final neckpiece will look and feel.

below A model tests the form and function of an unusual bangle.

below Simple paper, plastic, and brass foil models of tree rings are made and coloured where appropriate.

technical solutions Model making is especially important when it comes to testing technical theories. It is easy to make assumptions about crucial aspects of a design that rely on complex technical solutions. Making a technical model will enable you to pre-empt difficulties that might otherwise arise during the fabrication of the final piece, and avoid expensive mistakes. It also lets you test your skills.

Technical models need not be over-worked; try to identify the necessary tests to avoid spending time on superfluous detail. As with sketching, the first stage in model making is to define the purpose – what it is that you want to investigate. This might be the jointing system, the function of a closure, the weight of a piece, or the way a form fits the body. It is essential to focus on these questions so that you can decide how you should make your model.

materials Almost any material can be considered for model making. Wire armatures can be used with modelling clay for building three-dimensional forms, while simple paper and card cutouts can be used to explore shape. The photocopier can be used to reduce and enlarge as well as to duplicate. Base metals are a cheap alternative to precious ones for technical models. When considering making a model, try to assess whether it is necessary to use materials or processes that might cause the making of the model to be labour intensive – choose processes and materials that will best explain and explore the reason for your model to prevent this aspect of design from becoming a chore as it is a very useful stage of the design process.

right Various related forms are modelled in bark, concrete, and silver so that the aesthetic of the forms and design devices can be assessed.

below The process of model making is thoroughly recorded; photographs of models tested on the body are accompanied by notes and sketches, along with paper templates so that the forms can be easily repeated.

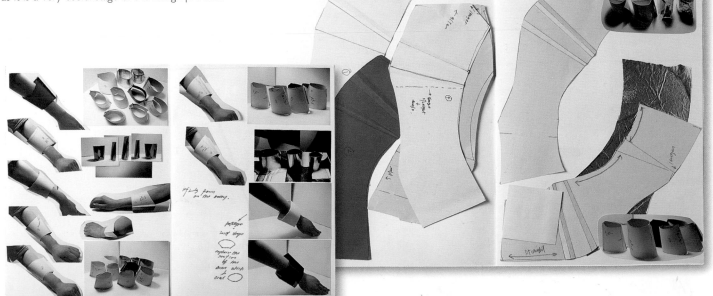

fabrication

Fabrication is the making stage, the physical realisation of a design through the use of the appropriate skills and materials.

from design to reality The fabrication of jewellery is obviously a significant stage of the design process, as without the end product the design is no more than an unproven theory. Occasionally fabrication is not the ultimate stage – the design is an end in itself. However, it is generally the aim of most designers to see their work realised.

To be able to design really well it is argued that a designer should have at least a basic command and understanding of the skills that would be required to fabricate their designs (see Craft Skills, pages 18–19). Through making you will learn about the possibilities of materials and processes, not only enabling you to design more effectively, but also helping you to avoid problems that could occur during fabrication.

If you intend to employ others to fabricate your designs you must give a clear, realistic brief. This will help to avoid disappointment and reduce the likelihood of fabrication costs exceeding your expectations.

above This mokumé gane brooch is made of copper and titanium. A technique like mokumé gane looks very appealing but does require considerable expertise.

right These pins are made of precious metal and gemstones. A high level of skill is required for designs to be made crisp, accurate and well finished.

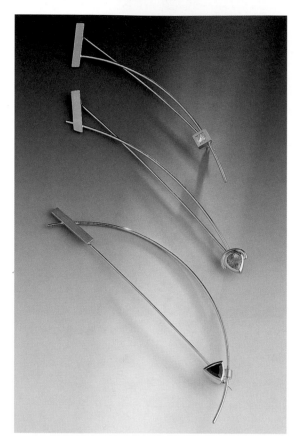

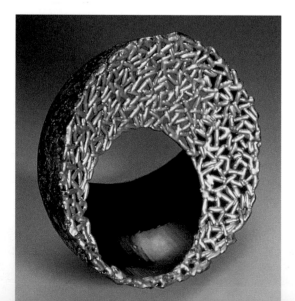

left To fabricate this fantastic design, titled 'The Moon', specialist lacquering skills are combined with innovative use of silver and gold powder.

being in control There are a number of ways in which the fabrication of jewellery is likely to happen. Unique, one-of-a-kind pieces will either be made by the designer, or a jeweller will be commissioned. In the latter case, detailed drawings and specifications would be required, and good communication between maker and designer is vital if the design is to be executed to the designer's satisfaction. If multiple copies are to be made, the design might be fabricated in a small-scale, low-level production scenario, or the pieces might be made as part of a larger production run.

For low-level production there are a few processes that enable the designs to be reproduced in quantity, such as casting, electro forming, photoetching and laser

pricing

If you intend to commission a maker to fabricate your design, or if you are asked to provide a quote for a commission, the total cost of fabrication needs to be considered.

✳

A comprehensive quote should include the following:

- **metal** – price per gram or ounce
- **main stone** – price per carat, carat weight
- **secondary stones** – price per piece and collectively
- **design** – a fee to be charged if commission is not fabricated, or design is not approved
- **labour** – price per hour to include studio and workshop costs and tools
- **casting** – cost of mold, casting fee
- **fittings** – ear clips, cufflink backs, chain, clasps
- **outwork** – engraving, setting, enamelling, stringing or other specialist outwork
- **assay** – hallmarking
- **packaging** – box and packaging materials
- **post** – special delivery, cost of general mail
- **miscellaneous** – travel, specialist material, etc.
- **profit** – generally 50%–100% above total costs

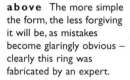

above The more simple the form, the less forgiving it will be, as mistakes become glaringly obvious – clearly this ring was fabricated by an expert.

above right The fabrication of a bracelet like this requires the designer's input, as much of the character of the piece is formed during this process.

below Fabrication can be a complex process, and models, notes and photographs will help as a record for future reference, especially when there is special tooling and assembly that needs testing before final fabrication in delicate or expensive materials.

cutting, to name but a few. These are specialist processes that require knowledge and experience, so time would need to be spent researching to understand and appreciate how these processes may be used to complement traditional craft skills. Larger production runs may involve expensive tooling; this way of working is more applicable to mass-market jewellery, as the cost of tooling is generally prohibitive for an individual designer.

Production processes can reduce the relative cost of manufacturing, but there is a strong possibility of compromise in the quality. To employ production processes it could still be necessary to make masters or a finished piece so that the results can be relied on. If you do neither of these yourself, but employ others, you will have to accept that they may not be able to interpret or handle your design as sensitively as you would like.

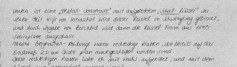

CHAPTER THREE
ELEMENTS OF DESIGN

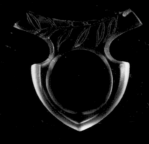

There are many ways a designer can make a piece of jewellery exciting and intriguing, however a design can easily become predictable and mundane. This may simply be because a few of the elements that can instill character have been overlooked.

Whatever the inspiration or concept behind a design, there are a number of important elements that should be considered during a comprehensive design development process. Take the time to consider shape, form, texture, colour, sensual and emotional impact, function, materials and process, to ensure that you do not miss valuable opportunities to improve, enhance and enrich your final design.

shape overview

The shapes we choose for our designs are of principal importance – they convey most of the initial visual impact of a piece of jewellery, and the way shapes are handled can alter the language of a piece in both subtle and significant ways.

Think of shape as a building block that can be used to ensure good aesthetic and visual balance. It can be treated as a frame or as a vehicle for more complex aspects of design, but care needs to be taken when embellishing the basic shape, or the design may become unnecessarily cluttered or overstated.

suitable characteristics It is essential to establish at the beginning what is required from your shape by referring to your concept – should the shape be bold, sleek, inviting, tactile, oriental, organic or something else? Draw a few basic shapes that might be suitable, and then consider how they might be developed to further express the concept and add character to your design.

To design effectively, you must try to understand the identity of a chosen shape. A square, for example, can

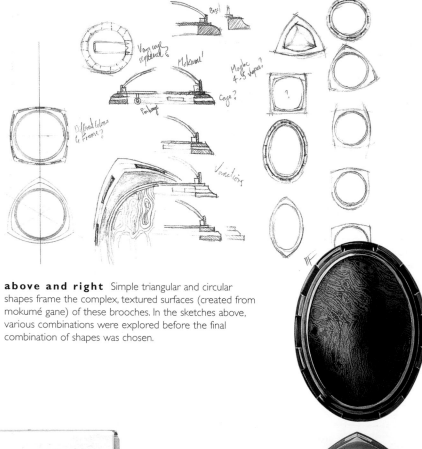

above and right Simple triangular and circular shapes frame the complex, textured surfaces (created from mokumé gane) of these brooches. In the sketches above, various combinations were explored before the final combination of shapes was chosen.

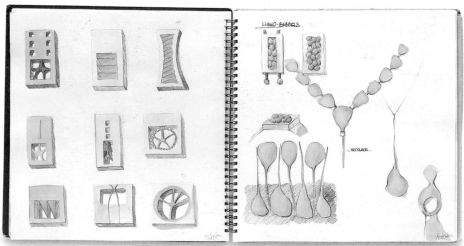

left Through these abstract studies of a lemon, the suitability of different shapes is considered. The designer has made a series of subtle changes to a basic four-sided shape, as well as alterations to the interior pattern. The simplicity of the frame means that the busy patterns do not have to compete for attention.

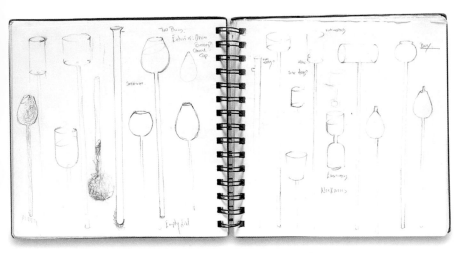

above These simple drawings explore a variety of shapes. Each has its own character, even though the differences in the shape are subtle. Open forms appear to be light containers, but by closing the symmetrical forms they are transformed into solid forms, reminiscent of hammers.

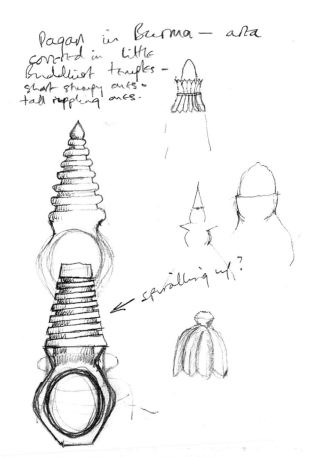

below and right
For this collection of silver jewellery, architectural sketches are developed and transformed into simple, elongated cone shapes. The surfaces of the cones are deeply scalloped to suggest the original architectural structures that inspired them.

be seen in simplistic terms as an orderly shape because it has equal sides, while a circle is infinite because it has no beginning or end. A triangle is a strong, centred, directional shape because it comes to a point. A simple, basic shape is easy to understand and work with because its impact and character can be easily modified by alterations to the edges or interiors so that its identity is changed.

With practice, you can tailor the properties of any shape to redefine its basic personality – try out a few simple alterations to see the effects that can be achieved. Don't be afraid to explore extremes; the most surprising and pleasing results frequently come through being daring and testing the boundaries.

shape case studies

When deciding on a shape, the sheer variety can be daunting, as every shape can be altered *ad infinitum*. Although this is clearly helpful for design development, it also means that sometimes it is difficult to halt the process or make definitive decisions.

capturing the orient When considering the shape for a design, it is a good idea to first narrow down options within a design brief so that you can focus more easily on what sort of shapes may be relevant. The brief for this ring required the designer to find a form that would evoke memories of the orient, and encapsulate its elegance and mystery.

To find a suitable shape, the designer thought about shapes that would suggest an oriental feel, and then spent time researching forms that are seen as specific to the orient, or that are generally associated with it. Sources of inspiration in this area are diverse, and included local architecture and architectural decoration, ceramics, textiles, flora and fauna and so on. The sweeping form of the finished piece is reminiscent of shapes seen in a Buddhist temple.

altering a shape's 'character': positive & negative space Once a shape has been developed to the point that the options have been narrowed down to only a few, the designer needs to be selective and decide which shapes are worth keeping. It is time to analyse the shapes and consider what makes one more appealing or successful than another. Testing those with the most potential as models helps this decision-making process.

You may end up finding a shape that suits your concept and design intent in a general sense, but is unsatisfactory in terms of function and aesthetics.

right This elegant ring is carved from Perspex. The theme is reinforced by the weeping willow leaves, which are often associated with the orient.

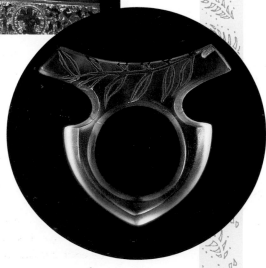

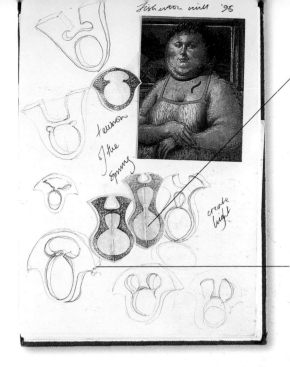

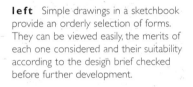

A simple photocopied template is used for making a model.

A model has been made out of Perspex to test the shape further.

The internal spaces define a critical, if subtle, shape, which affects the overall appearance of the shape.

Changing the proportions of a shape can significantly alter the impact of a design.

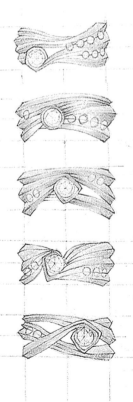

left Simple drawings in a sketchbook provide an orderly selection of forms. They can be viewed easily, the merits of each one considered and their suitability according to the design brief checked before further development.

An understanding of shape enables a designer to identify the various qualities that may make it inappropriate – it might seem too aggressive, crude or clumpy, for example – and manipulate the shape and its proportions to produce something more appealing and appropriate.

It is important to understand the way in which shapes can define both positive and negative space. The rings shown on this page rely heavily on negative spaces, which can either soften or emphasise the outer contours. The negative shape of the ring shank is generally round, but these ring designs also prove that this is not an absolute. By considering the shape of the negative space of a ring through which the finger passes, and extending this in conjunction with the external shape, the designer has created distinctive ring designs that are essentially two-dimensional.

above An assortment of drawings, templates, and models clearly shows the relationship between the various ring forms – the lines are swept outwards, or upwards and internal shapes are redefined.

below These design sketches couple a variety of bold and diminutive shapes, that are then either attached or removed from the main shape to act as decorative detail.

shape jeweller's showcase

'In 'Princess', basic organic or round forms are used to reflect the symmetry and beauty of the female form. Material, colour and shape have to be in harmony. Proportion is also very important – the different dimensions of the various components of the piece have to be in accord as well.' **jenny sauer**

'Princess' The design of the neckpiece is based on *The Seven Stories of the Seven Princesses*, written by Nizami in the 12th century. Each story is represented by a colour, day and star; this design is based on the story, 'What the Indian Princess Told on Saturday in the Black Saturn-Dome' – a story of unfulfilled love.

The eight inner fairy-forms, placed like a blossom that can be turned, symbolise dancing fairies, the main subject of the story. Their shape was developed from a personal interpretation of the fairy – female, translucent and light creatures, dancing, moving and beautiful like a flower. The materials are carefully chosen to introduce colour as an affirmation of various design elements; black steel and rubber are symbolic of night, blue chalcedony represents Saturn and white crystal, contrasting with the darker colours, signifies the light of the fairies.

opposite page The concept of the piece required the designer to find a definitive shape that would act as a symbolic device to describe the delicate, feminine qualities of a fairy, and to show how perfectly they are formed – the answer, a rounded, completely symmetrical shape. The background sketches show the various shapes the designer considered for the internal forms.

right This bold pendant form is made of chalcedony, crystal and surgical steel strung on rubber thread. The two-dimensional internal shapes are combined to make a three-dimensional object for the wearer to explore.

form overview

Jewellery is a three-dimensional discipline that relates directly to the mobile, variable, three-dimensional form of the body, with its curving, rounded shapes. Three-dimensional objects can offer a rich, visual and tactile experience, full of surprises and exciting changes as they are explored through 360 degrees.

inside and out   A good design is distinguished from an ordinary one by attention to detail, both large and small, so always check that you have considered all aspects of form and are conscious of the potential of the different faces of a piece throughout the design process. This helps to achieve a cohesive design in which all aspects of form have been addressed.

Form is not just about the parts of a piece that can be seen. In a good design the back of a piece should

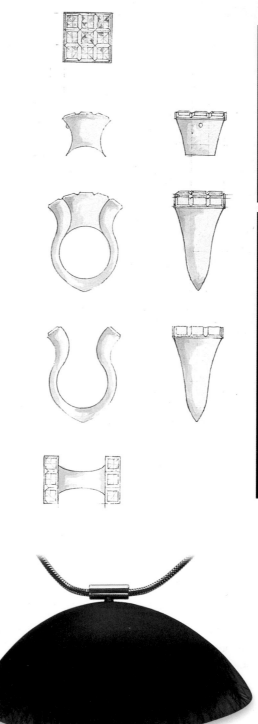

above   Shaped sheets of coloured paper are stacked to form a solid, cylindrical bangle. Looking from above, the form falls away from the rim to give the centre a gentle, conical look that makes it both visually interesting and physically satisfying.

right   Three-dimensional form is used to manipulate the degree of translucency of this resin pendant. The resin is carved into a curvaceous form, thinning from a full body to a knife edge at the base – the internal texture becomes visible as the form thins, and the translucency of the resin increases.

above, centre and left   Drawings indicate different views of a two-part ring, and show it both fully assembled and separated. The measured drawings allow the forms to be visualised and checked before the design is finalised and the ring is fabricated.

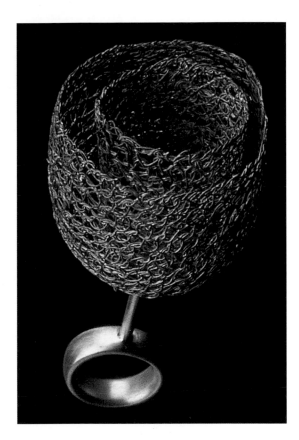

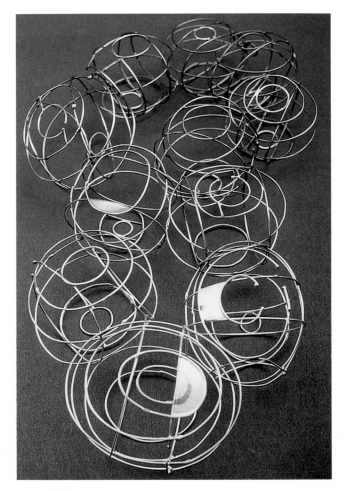

left The outer voluminous form on top of this silver ring acts as a container for a smaller form that nestles inside it. The smaller form adds depth and further interest to the design.

right These airy, three-dimensional forms are made from wire. Lines and intersections create different patterns according to the angle at which they are viewed. Tiny glimpses of solid forms that relate to the linear structure are suggested by sheet detail.

below This pair of silver rings shows how three-dimensional forms can be defined by line or a solid surface. The delicate bell form is worn so that it is protected and enclosed by the wirework ring.

complement the front. To find that the back is a thing of beauty in itself is like discovering a secret – one that will make a piece infinitely more satisfying and memorable.

two dimensions into three When you begin designing, your drawings may be rather two-dimensional, because you are likely to be drawing from a single viewpoint. Form is difficult to convey on paper, so it is important to learn how to draw in three dimensions, using contour and perspective. Measured drawing is an accurate and relatively simple way of exploring form: by projecting the shape into three dimensions, the different elevations of a piece can be connected to check that decisions about detailing and proportions are sympathetic and plausible.

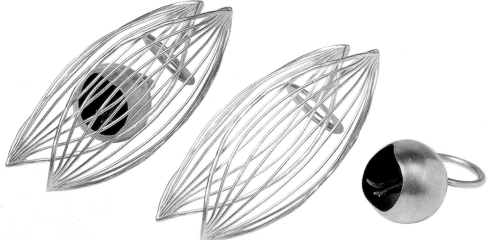

form case studies

In films and literature, characters are damned as being two-dimensional if they are predictable and under-developed. In jewellery, two-dimensional work can suffer the same fate, as it is harder to engage the wearer when a piece lacks the added character that well-conceived form can offer.

realising form When asked to imagine a three-dimensional form we often think of solid forms with solid surfaces, so it is useful to make a model that helps with visualisation. Once you have a physical object, you can either develop the design directly through model-making, or you can make a skeletal model and put flesh on the bones by drawing in the detail or covering the structure.

Conversely, three-dimensional form need not always be realised as a solid object; volume can be thought of as defining a space rather than filling it in, as in the ring shown above.

Designers often aim to imagine how a three-dimensional form would look if it were defined by a number of lines. Contour lines help to realise a form that is three-dimensional, while at the same time allowing the internal space to be visualised. This is a useful exercise to practise because it encourages you to consider the volume and internal form, as well as the profile, of a piece.

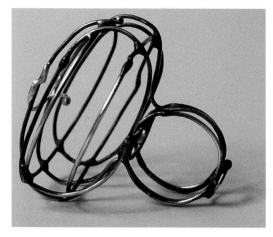

above This ring model uses lines of oxidised silver wire to define a voluminous cushion form that is intended to be the central feature of the final design.

right Contour lines show the curvature of a form and help the designer to visualise how a piece might undulate. Working in perspective also provides useful, if slightly restricted, views of the piece.

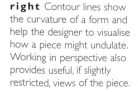

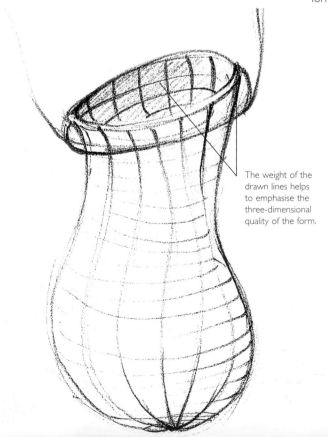

The weight of the drawn lines helps to emphasise the three-dimensional quality of the form.

form in motion Designing form that is not rigid is a good way of introducing movement, as well as an interactive quality, to a piece. The silver bracelet (below) has been conceived so that the form alters significantly depending on whether it is laid flat on a surface or suspended. When lying flat the piece appears basically two-dimensional, but once lifted, the numerous individual spines are released to spiral freely, redefining and transforming the bracelet's form.

Similarly, the pair of red and black bangles (right) combines hard, inflexible metal with tactile, mobile ribbon so that the form of the bangle is constantly changing when it is worn – and even when it is static, the form is never exactly the same twice.

The silver tips act as ballasts that affect the form and also finish off the ends of the ribbons.

The flexible ribbons are soft enough to allow an arm to pass through them, but stiff enough to stand upright.

left and above This pair of bangles includes silver-tipped ribbons held in geometric, two-dimensional frames. The ribbons fall randomly toward the centre of the frame, so the form of the resting piece will always be slightly different.

Using dissimilar materials creates contrast in texture and colour.

left and right When laid flat, this bracelet looks rather like an elegant, snaking form made of neatly ordered, silver twigs.

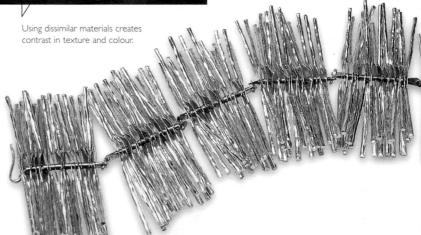

form jeweller's showcase

This piece stemmed from my interest in horses, and their saddlery in particular. Saddles provide a rich source of research material due to their dramatic form, weight and scale.

beth gilmour

saddle bangle A saddle is designed to fit the body of a horse so that it shields the horse's spine from the weight of the rider and allows the rider to sit comfortably.

To enable this to happen, there is a negative space that runs above the horse's spine. Beth Gilmour noticed this space when riding and realised that it is hidden from most angles. She then set out to create a large-scale jewellery piece that defines volume and negative spaces in a similar manner to the saddle.

The location of the piece was determined by a desire to link oppositely curving planes of the wrist and hip, as well as to reflect the way riders carry their saddles – balanced against the hip. The unlikely materials used were determined by a one-week deadline: the bangle was carved from polystyrene, coated with a sealant, and then sanded, creating a hard, cold finish.

opposite page The bold form of the bangle is inspired by the satisfying curves of a saddle – a functional object that balances pressure and contact so that neither comfort nor function are compromised. The necklace and brooch are comprised of rounded forms covered in leather. Here and there, a tiny glimpse of the lustre of a pearl can be seen through a few small slits in the leather.

left and above The cool, white form of this dramatic sculptural armpiece fits the arm like a second skin. It sits snugly against the hip so that the negative space that frames part of the arm is hidden within the form.

texture overview

Jewellery is a tactile medium, designed to be handled and worn, so the way it feels is clearly an important element. The term 'texture' is generally thought of as relating to the sense of touch alone, however, it is usually a visual experience as well. The surface finish of a piece can lift it from the ordinary to the extraordinary because of the way in which it stimulates and entertains our senses.

evocative textures and materials

People often think of jewellery as being highly polished, but although a mirror finish has its place, there are many other interesting textural surfaces, and texture should never be overlooked in the design process. Metal, the most commonly used material in jewellery design, has a hard surface, but through applying appropriate processes it can be made to appear soft, inviting, and even velvety.

Most of the materials used in jewellery making present opportunities for exploring and exploiting a

right and below The inspiration for textures can come from anywhere, from the natural world to man- or machine-made objects. Visual and technical journals are useful tools for recording visual and physical textures for future reference.

a feather's texture speaks of both delicacy and strength.

right Dyed paper cord and felt are used to make an exuberant and highly textural neckpiece. It is visually attractive because of its texture, colour and form, and it also invites tactile enquiry because of the unusual materials used.

wide range of exciting textures, however it is important when choosing a material and texture to consider whether they will wear well for the intended lifespan of the piece, whether that be a month, a year, a decade, or a lifetime.

visual language Our perception of texture is ingrained as part of a common visual language – we expect an object to be old if it has a tarnished surface or is covered in the familiar green patina caused by weathering. This kind of knowledge is useful in creating pieces that evoke a particular response. Physical and visual texture can be readily employed to imitate commonly recognised surfaces, and therefore to reinforce the design intention. For example, a silver surface can be etched into stripes, gold-plated and oxidised to suggest a tiger's pelt – it may not feel like fur, but the visual connection is readily made.

above and right The unusual, key-shaped bangle uses patination to highlight lettering, and the carefully applied surface of green and oxide gives the feeling of antiquity. In the related ring, with a secret to unlock, patination is used in a different way to create a visual texture that attracts the eye and emphasises the shape.

right For this simple, round brooch, a delicate visual texture reminiscent of dyed silk is cleverly made in metal using the mokumé gane technique and patination.

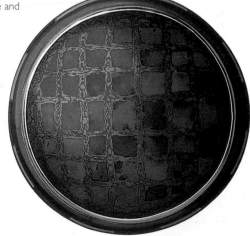

texture case studies

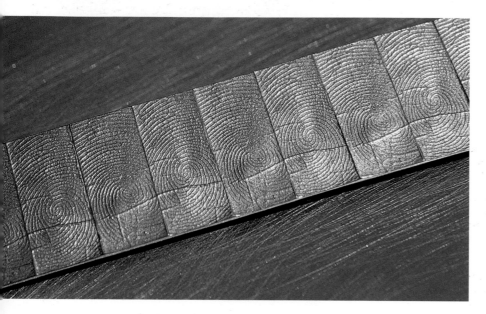

left The texture of the
this brooch is a direct
reference to skin, itself the
very means of our accessing
the sense of touch – a good
example of how texture can
be used as a vehicle for the
concept, as well as being a
decorative element.

right This clever bangle
protects a vulnerable
texture in a 'container'
form. By exploiting the
translucency of the material,
the texture can still be seen
through the smooth surface.

below This pendant form
with a hidden bell appeals to
the senses of sight, sound,
and touch.

Texture can be a sublime experience, where our tactile
senses can revel in the delicious or delicate, or it can
be a feast for the eyes, to entrance and enthrall.
Whatever the effect, texture is a powerful element
of design, and whatever the surface texture may be,
it should not be arbitrary.

inviting textures Jewellery is often thought of
as an extension of ourselves, and handling a familiar
piece of jewellery can be a means of reassurance, giving
a sense of well-being and comfort. Acknowledging this,
the designer of the pendant (right) appeals directly to
people's attraction to tactile objects. The effect is
emphasised through contrast – the smooth, clean,
cylindrical body looks heavy and fits into the hand, while
the domed base, with its gentle, playful dimples, offers
a different textural and tactile experience. The domed
base hides a bell inside, combining texture and sound
to give the design extra sensual appeal.

The perfect line and
surface create an
industrial look, but is
nonetheless appealing
and begs to be handled.

The texture of the
dimpled base acts
as a visual lure that
prevents the eye from
being lulled by the
clean surface and form.

practical considerations You should consider whether the surface of a material would benefit from a textural finish in practical terms. Bearing in mind that a high polish is one of the most difficult surfaces to achieve, applying a texture can be doubly advantageous.

On the other hand, textured surfaces can be difficult to clean, and depending on where on the body the piece is to be worn, it may be subject to abrasion that can cause the texture to fade.

To the designer, a surface that is susceptible to damage and difficult to maintain might hold a special attraction; it can add the dimension of fragility to a piece. A designer who chooses to use such surfaces needs to rationalise the pros and cons of this fragility, and consider means of protecting the surface from reasonable wear. The pieces of jewellry shown here represent designs in which the protection of the surface and texture has been considered and incorporated as an integral design feature.

The subtly textured silver tendrils add visual interest, contrast and movement, and protect the woven thread of the bangle form.

The woven thread becomes the vehicle for colour and pattern.

right Coloured thread and hammered silver are used to create contrasting textures that entertain the eye.

bottom left Oriental lacquerwork adorns the surface of a silver ring titled 'Rotate Galax'. The extruded silver frame helps to protect the delicate surface from damage, and also accentuates the design imagery.

below This series of rings uses texture both as a protective and decorative device.

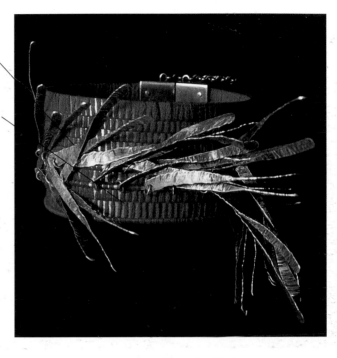

The polished, raised areas emphasise and protect the texture.

The freshly pickled, vulnerable white in the valleys contrasts with the grey sheen of the polished silver.

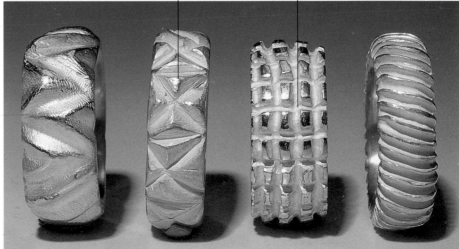

texture jeweller's showcase

" I believe that our ability to contemplate and concentrate is deteriorating as a result of a fast-moving, highly technological environment, and that we have become impatient creatures. "

mikala djorup

white flower ring Inspired by thoughts on movement, discovery and repetition, the white flower ring challenges the tendency towards impatience through jewellry that demands attention and interaction – and through this, the relationship between wearer and object is reinforced. The moving stems jostle each other with the movement of the hand, and create a faint sound to make a private place – a compact 'finger garden'. With time, the movement of the flowers would become familiar to the wearer.

Form is created by making a surface through the repetition of the flower shapes. This form disappears and reappears, but because the elements are all slightly different, the surface comes alive through the constantly changing juxtaposition. The aim of the work is to include movement that creates an experience of discovery and joy of the unexpected. The movements are subtle, and can be appreciated privately or shared.

opposite page The silver in this neckpiece and bracelet is annealed and then pickled to look white, or scratched, as if it is not yet ready for public appearance. The interaction between wearer and piece will result in surface changes – wear will reveal the shiny metal surface where the piece is in contact with the skin, connecting the piece to the wearer. The repeated ovals in the silver and plastic necklace are strung in strict order, but this is only glimpsed, as the ovals lie randomly around the neck. In the background, sketchbook drawings of carefully plotted lines map the contours of delicate textural surfaces.

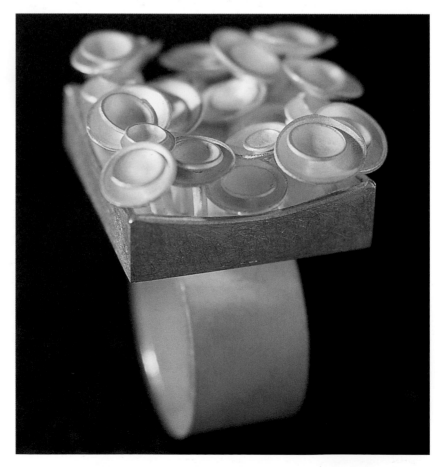

right Simple geometrical shapes form the basis of this ring, and texture, tactility and clean shapes provide the 'silence' to explore these qualities.

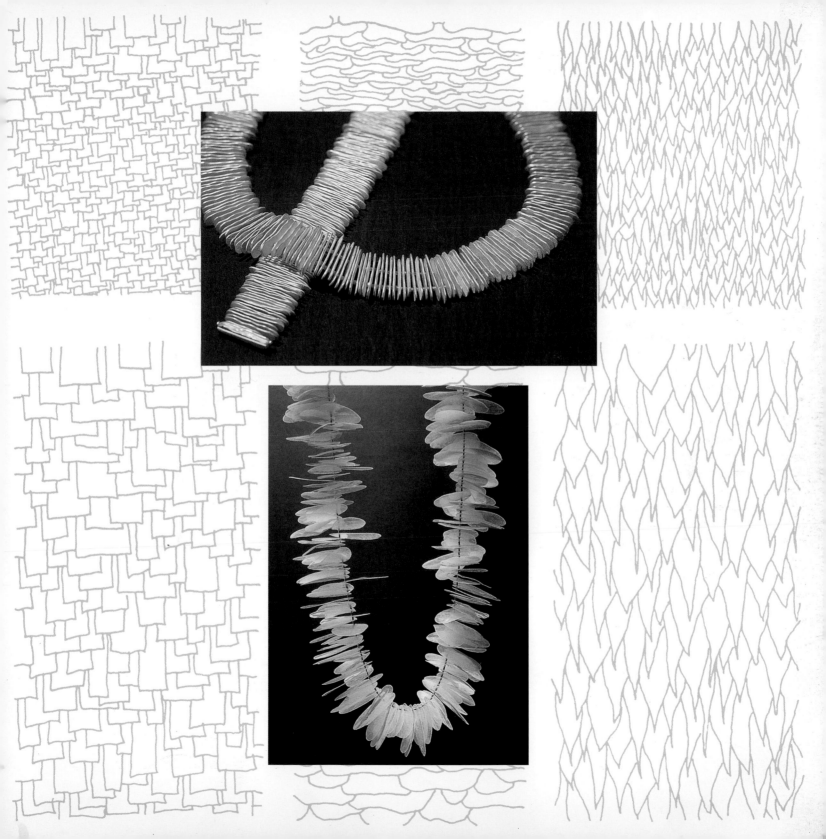

colour overview

Colour is one of the most immediate and effective ways of attracting attention to work – we are a visually sensitive species, and colour is a very important stimulus. Colour is a useful device for enriching jewellery and enhancing the must-have factor. By offering a design in a choice of colours, a designer has the opportunity to customise the work according to the whims of the client or seasonal fashion trends.

tradition and innovation In past centuries, jewellery was a mainly metal-based discipline. As jewellery was associated in many cultures with prosperity, precious metals such as silver and gold were the primary materials used. Colour was added by the inclusion of stones or coloured beads, or through enamelling. Seeds, feathers and other brightly coloured objects were no doubt used as well, but these were generally a poor-man's substitute for the valuable materials that were only accessible to the wealthy.

Scientific advances have given contemporary jewellery a much wider palette of materials. In the 1980s titanium came in and went out of fashion, while plastic has gone from strength to strength since its introduction; because it is constantly being developed, it has a lot more possibilities than titanium, which quickly became ordinary.

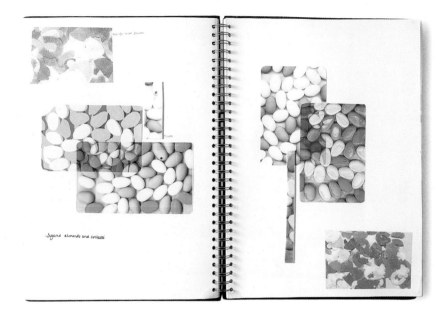

above The springtime colours of the pink and white sugared almonds, here seen in a visual journal, could be used as the inspiration for a future collection of bridal or fashion jewellry designs.

below right The vibrant blue in this feather brooch, set with diamonds, is created using anodised titanium.

left A pair of silver pendants is made even more attractive by lustrous, deep red seed-like beads.

left Resin is cast into quirky, curvaceous forms to make a neckpiece of opaque, translucent and transparent green. The strands of dyed nylon filament embedded in the transparent forms add visual texture as well as colour to the piece.

right Humble paper is transformed through cutting and assembly with silver to make a collection of vivid bangles. The layers of orange, red and pink are subtly varied in places to add additional interest and visual allure.

Original ways of including colour in jewellery are continually being explored by designers who aim to establish their design style through explorations into unusual materials and techniques.

the language of colour The way people feel and react to colour is to a large extent personal; however, certain colours are generally understood to have particular 'personalities' – blue, for example, is believed to be calming, and red aggressive, or suggestive of passion or lust.

right These wonderful, pod-like forms are richly coloured on the inside. The muted exteriors appear to be simple, organic shapes, while the interiors are little treasure-troves of colour that demand attention.

Culture also plays a part in people's attitudes toward different colours: a Western bride would be unlikely to wear red at the altar, whereas a Chinese bride may well do so because in traditional Chinese culture red is an auspicious colour linked with religion.

In the West, colour can also be a metaphor for the seasons and the cycle of life: light and pale colours indicate spring and youth; intense or bright colours symbolise summer and maturity; dark and faded colours, autumn and old age; and white or washed-out colours, winter and death.

Knowing what a colour means in a particular context allows you to focus on how it can be used in combination with form, texture and other relevant factors, to make the design intention of a piece more readily realised and understood.

colour case studies

Understanding how colour will affect the visual impact of a piece is essential. Colour is a powerful tool, and if used with sensitivity, it can be a useful and sophisticated mouthpiece for a designer.

changing a colour's impact Colour should not be used arbitrarily. It is essential to make colour studies that explore different effects. If opaque, a colour will probably have a stronger impact than if it is translucent; if it is graded it can be made to suggest form and movement; and if there is a blanket of one colour, then the effect is more static. Graded colour is generally more natural and organic than blanket colour, which tends to be associated with the manmade.

Take the time to examine colours, to see how the visual balance and aesthetics of a piece can be changed by different shades, variations and intensities of colour. These visual journals illustrate how important the exploration of colour is for many designers, even at the earliest stages of design development.

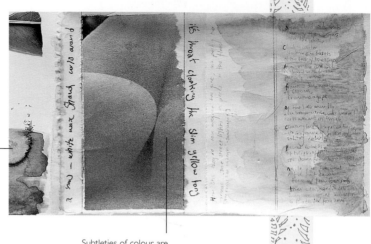

The inky blue/black of the watercolour paint and feather work in unexpected harmony with the warm pastel colours on the opposite page.

Subtleties of colour are explored through abstracting a small part of a larger image.

A button and other small objects whose colours relate to the printed composition are collected for potential inclusion in future designs.

Alongside the image the designer has copied down an inspirational poem by Stevie Smith: '... Bricks, slates, paving stones are coloured/And it has been raining now./They shine.'

The inclusion of small areas of contrasting colour distract and entertain the eye.

right and above
Colour studies in a visual journal or sketchbook are a means of recording and trying out combinations and compositions in colour that can be translated into a jewellery design. Vibrant reds can be used to draw in the eye, and suggest passion and energy, while a composition of muted pastels is more likely to soothe the eye and promote calm.

key points

The range of alternative materials used in contemporary jewellery design means that choice in colour is virtually limitless

✳

Consider how the physical surface affects colour. For example, a shiny surface that reflects a sheen will have a different affect to the same colour in matte.

✳

A colour's character and impact can be easily altered by changing the amount and intensity.

using traditional and alternative materials

Enamelling is traditionally a popular way of incorporating colour in jewellery. However, it is a difficult technique to handle, so you should take the time to make samples so that you can test the colours and examine the effect before working on the final piece – this can save considerable time and energy in the long run.

It is useful to consider alternative materials as a means of bringing colour to jewellery; by using materials that are more often associated with other industries or disciplines, such as Formica and plastic laminates from interior design, or tassels and trimming as used in upholstery or the fashion industry, a designer can add both colour and interest. Whether colour is introduced through the application of enamel or the use of dyed paper, it is the way the material and colour are used and applied that will define the piece as traditional or contemporary.

below Combining hard and soft materials is a useful way of including colour and visual texture – the inclusion of tassels brings movement and energy to a pair of dramatic earrings for the fashion market.

right These two related brooches show how colour can affect the character of a piece. The bold red panel is set so that the form is proud and dominant, in keeping with the 'personality' of the colour, while the panel of quiet, pastel tones is inverted in a more passive stance that is more in sympathy with its gentle character.

above Good designers are conscious of the effects of colour, and are careful not to use colour indiscriminately. The balance of colour in this neckpiece is designed so that it complements the texture and form.

right Enamelled panels in a technical journal explore various combinations of colour and ways of handling the technique.

Titled 'At night the mountain range glows red', this ghostly affect was achieved through bleeding coloured enamels.

Repeated firing turned the silver flux from a pearly white to a gentle sea green colour.

colour jeweller's showcase

" Acrylic has excellent working qualities, and while initially attracted to the material by the colour it offers, I currently produce work centred on its ability to act as a receptacle for light – wearable pieces with a distinct element of fun. **"**

adam paxon

wrap-around ring-to-brooch These pieces are intended to tease out the hidden qualities in materials – through laminating, forming and carving acrylic, its colours are blended so that the designer can discover subtleties of newly enriched colour. Inspired by the way that light can change the character and colour of a piece, Adam Paxon has designed pieces in which light is manipulated so that it is either contained and guided through the piece, or projected outwards over the wearer's skin or garment.

The gleaming finish has a wet look and reflective surfaces help to charge the colour, accentuating the erotic and sensuous quality of the pieces so that they appear ready to burst with ripeness. The forms are designed to appear as if they have organically grown or erupted out of a garment, or to look as if they are resting before they scurry over a shoulder.

As the designer developed the work the pieces evolved to become more and more like 'creatures to wear'. The brooch attachments are enclosed within the form to avoid confusing the brooch's appearance or character, and the integral fittings give the forms a convincing dual identity. The inclusion of movement in the form suggests small animal movements – breathing, quivering or foraging – as well as having erotic or sexual parallels.

opposite page In many of Adam Paxon's pieces the value of the object is increased by the method of attachment, which is designed to be in harmony with the piece. The jewellery can be worn as rings, brooches or neckpieces, and add a burst of colour wherever they are situated.

above These wearable, sculptural ring-to-brooches have an element of fun that manages to skirt novelty and steer the wearer and viewer towards other, more suggestive contexts.

five senses overview

When designing, never forget that you have five senses – sight, touch, sound, smell and taste. Jewellery obviously engages some of these more than others, but by considering all of them, it is possible to discover design opportunities that might not have otherwise been obvious.

taste, smell and sound For obvious reasons, taste is very rarely included as a sensual experience in jewellery design. However, there have been conceptual pieces designed with the idea in mind that they could be consumed rather than last for eternity.

right These unusual bar rings nestle securely on the finger as a flip flop does on the foot. The wearer can add perfume to the colourful silk inserts to create a personal fragrant experience.

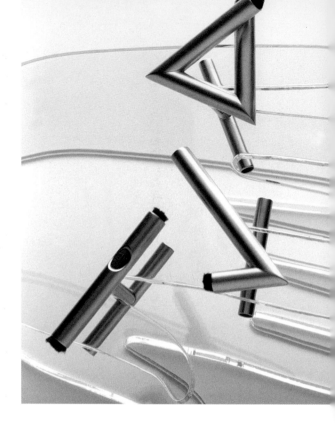

below left The elegant silver pendants of this neckpiece gently strike against each other with the motion of the wearer's body to create a sound that would undoubtedly become familiar and pleasing to the wearer. Because the pendants are handcrafted rather than machine-made, each neckpiece made would have its own unique audio signature.

below This unusual collection of rings is made to contain a carefully selected range of visually delightful food, offering a rare opportunity to engage the sense of taste through jewellery.

Smell, likewise, is not usually seen as an important factor in contemporary jewellery, but it should not be ruled out. In past centuries jewellery was often made specifically as containers for fragrant plants, such as lavender or rose, to hide a variety of unpleasant smells, including those of the body.

Sound can be inadvertently added to jewellery, as objects that come into contact with each other are likely to create some sort of noise. Different forms and materials will affect the sound that occurs when objects strike each other, and an awareness of this enables you to ensure that the resulting noise is an additional pleasure rather then an unwanted irritation. You might even consider making this a primary feature of a design, rather than merely a by-product of the piece.

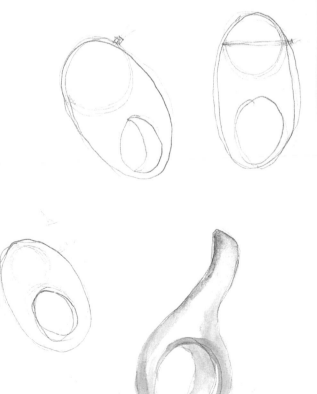

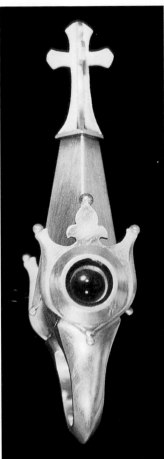

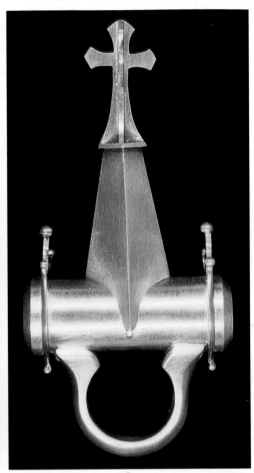

above and left
Options for a temptation ring were considered, including an outlandish tongue form, before the church design was settled on. In the final design the temptation is to look into the church through the viewfinder. The tempted discovers a transparency or 'stained glass window' depicting Adam and Eve.

sight and touch The way in which jewellery impacts on us visually is obviously the most important factor to be considered when designing – if you fail to engage your audience visually, you are unlikely to have the opportunity to excite their other senses.

The tactile quality of a piece is very important, as it can easily affect how we respond to the piece, and whether or not we find it pleasing to wear – a ring, for example, is usually polished on the inside so that it feels silky against the finger. Handling a sharp, prickly object, on the other hand, can be disturbing initially, but if the sensation is designed to be a controlled or limited experience it can also be surprisingly enjoyable.

five senses jeweller's showcase

'This bold and graphic group of pieces is connected thematically by the senses, each piece celebrating one of the five. How the individual perceives and responds to the five senses is important, because this differs from person to person. For me, the senses are about enquiry and discovery.' **suzanne potter**

enquiry and discovery The inspiration for these pieces comes from a wide range of visual and tactile sources – from unspoiled nature to utilitarian machines. The resulting forms are then developed and honed to produce essentially abstract forms and shapes that reflect a modern, clean aesthetic.

The playful quality of the work is an important feature of the designs, and the pieces reveal their secrets and come alive through interaction. Experiencing the work through handling it is an important aspect of the design, because each form has been made to hold its own surprise that stimulates the senses. Emotional thoughts and desires are triggered by the senses, so by taking familiar sights, smells, sounds, tastes and tactile experiences, and presenting them in an unusual context, the sensual experience is emphasised and enhanced.

opposite page The mirror in the 'Eyespy' ring (top left) is so small that the viewer can only see their eye. The fingerprint earrings, 'Pressure Points', (top right) are a reminder of earlobes. The 'Holding Noise' rings (bottom left) incorporate sounds based on those of percussion instruments. The portholes in the miniature containers (bottom right) reveal everyday food substances, salt and sugar, begging the question: which one is which?

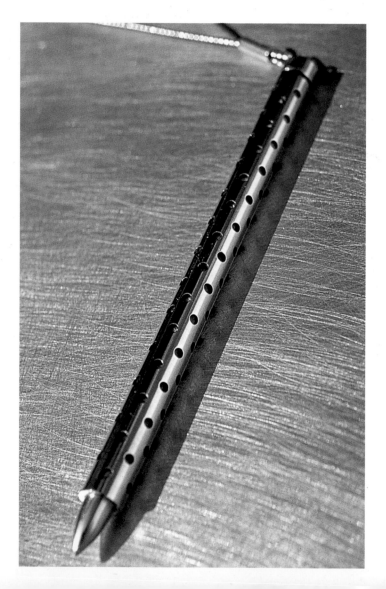

right The pendant form in this neckpiece, titled 'Lemon Sunshine', holds felt that has been impregnated with lemon-scented aromatherapy oil. The oil exudes a fresh, cleansing, vibrant and uplifting smell, designed to evoke a bright and sunny mood. The container is based on the elegant, streamlined exhaust of a garbage truck!

emotion overview

Jewellery has been used to appeal to our emotions for centuries, and a look at the history of jewellery design reveals pieces that have inspired reverence, fear, joy, laughter and sorrow.

horror Some emotions are personal, while others are shared by groups of people. For example, fear of spiders (arachnophobia) is relatively common, and even those who are not actually phobic may still feel uncomfortable when facing a large, hairy spider. The inclusion of elements that might cause people discomfort or uneasiness can be a good way of attracting attention to a design, as people tend to be drawn to that which is fearsome or disturbing.

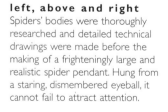

CHAIN SOLDERED INTO TUBE GIVES SOLIDITY TO CATCH

catch

RIVET WIRE SOLDERED INTO ROD

hole for 0.9mm

2mm   1mm

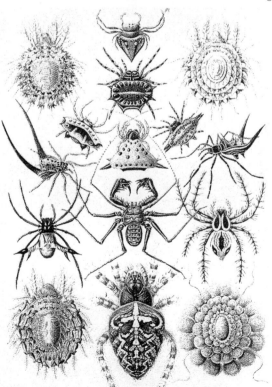

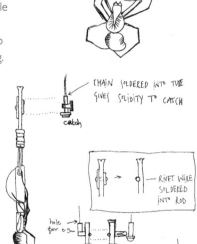

left, above and right
Spiders' bodies were thoroughly researched and detailed technical drawings were made before the making of a frighteningly large and realistic spider pendant. Hung from a staring, dismembered eyeball, it cannot fail to attract attention.

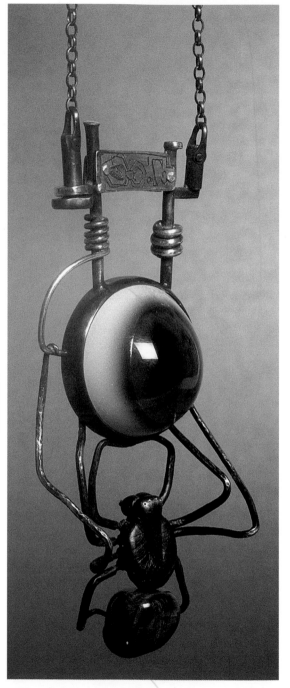

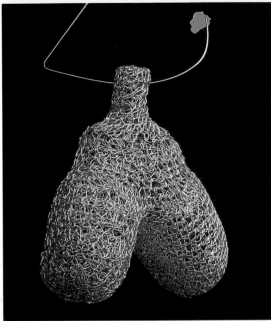

left The shape of this brooch speaks for itself, but the title 'The Jewels' confirms the unbelievable. The pendant is crafted from silver and steel to make a provocative, tongue-in-cheek piece of jewellery.

right A cat fishing on the edge of a bowl, and a predator fish with a human face, are a pair of simple, endearing images that were considered during the development of a ring design. The designer appears not to take life – or jewellry – too seriously.

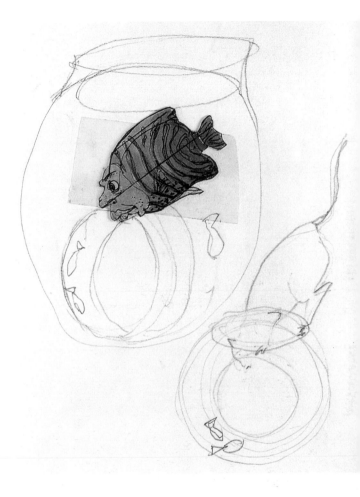

humour

humour Humour is another human quality that is often exploited in jewellery. A design that includes humour and has the ability to make people smile will generally be appealing.

There are many ways of provoking mirth in jewellery. Think of jewellery that makes you smile or laugh as a visual joke. You might consider using a title that helps explain the joke. Ideally, however, the visual image should convey sufficient information for the joke to be understood, with the title merely confirming the punchline – otherwise, as it is not always possible for

above The three adorable bunnies in this brooch are a sure-fire recipe for producing a smile, but the title 'Menagerie à Trois', twists the image of innocence by adding innuendo. As in many good jokes, it is the unexpected that provokes laughter.

the viewer to know the title, the joke might fall on deaf ears.

Jewellery is generally regarded as a serious subject, so a design that incorporates humour has the advantage of surprise. It should not be hard to find themes that will raise a smile, but because jewellery is a small canvas, you may need to keep the idea simple – children's humour, puns and familiar humourous and comic images are all useful sources of inspiration.

emotion jeweller's showcase

" While the pieces I make are very personal to me, I am happy that people can interpret them differently. It is important to me to make pieces of jewellery that are fun to wear, and a conversation point for the wearer. "

sarah graveson

'do dogs dream of chasing comets?' The initial inspiration for this
series was the story of Laika, the dog sent into space in the late 1950s by the Soviet Union. This was then combined with images from science-fiction films that had trickled into the designer's subconscience – dogs were visualised fully equipped with zero-gravity space boots, oxygen tank and helmet, whizzing around space, hopping onto the moon and riding comets. The 'Dogs in Space' theme widened as the designer changed the context from outer space to the space that is a dog's environment.

Getting a puppy turned Sarah's life upside down, creating a whole gamut of emotions that she eventually used in her jewellery designs. As part of the design process a great deal of research was done: pictures and articles were collected, and the artist made her own drawings from life – either from actual dogs or at museums and from videos. This brooch was based on combined images of the puppy's obsessions, such as chasing helicopters, balls, bees and so on, with imagined images of the puppy's dreams as she lay twitching and moaning, with legs moving, as if running in her sleep.

right With its cheerful imagery and lively colours, this charming and humourous brooch provokes a smile, and not just from those who have, or have had, a dog in their life.

opposite page
Continuing with the depiction of the canine world and the 'Dogs in Space' theme, the pin (top right) is titled 'Haley Toesis' – an amusing double entendre. Models made during the design process explore other facets of canine life and character.

function overview

A good jewellery designer should take a holistic approach to his or her work so that all aspects of the design are considered and included as part of the overall design intention. The function of a piece should therefore be considered not as a separate, practical concern, but as potentially integral to the overall design.

inventive solutions The function of a piece may be a simple issue, such as the need for a catch to open and close a neck chain, but in some cases it can be more challenging – for example, a ring might be required to light up when a trigger is activated by a finger passed though the form.

If your design is heavily biased towards function, it is important to explore various possibilities and learn more about that function. If, for example, your piece is to act as a fastening, then brainstorming and researching different ways of fastening will inevitably turn up a number of options – buttons, safety pins, locks and latches are just a few possibilities – and will feed the design process.

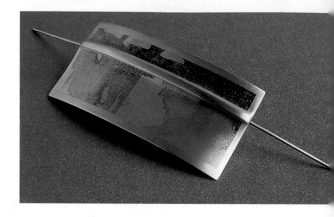

right The pin on this simple silver brooch contributes significantly to the balance of the composition and visual aesthetic, rather than just being a functional addition.

One way to broaden your knowledge is to explore other fields; looking to jewellery alone for solutions is very limiting and restrictive. Instead, think of all the different methods of fastening there are – in the kitchen, on clothing, in industry and so on – and then consider how you might translate these solutions into a jewellery format.

below Changing the size of a ring has always been a problem for jewellery designers. This series of drawings explores various ways of changing the size of a ring so that the function of the piece is an essential element, integral to the design.

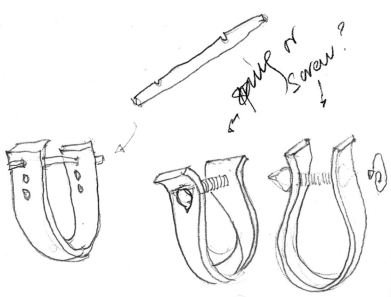

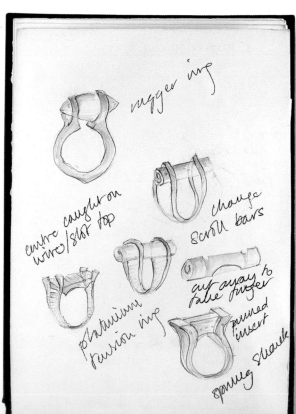

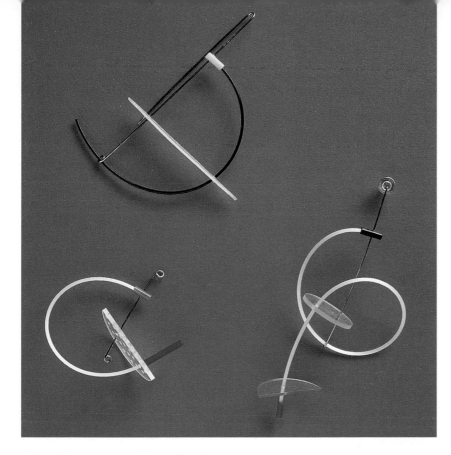

above The steel pins in this set of brooches are an important element of the design – the wires used for the pins help to describe the shape and also serve a functional purpose.

function and aesthetics In many cases functional elements must be included in a design to enable satisfactory fabrication. One example is hollow work, which often requires airholes to be included to avoid explosions during soldering. These need only be small holes drilled into the form, but rather than having them only fulfil a utilitarian purpose, a better solution might be to incorporate them into the design so that they become a feature, rather than a potential eyesore.

Often the only way you can make a piece function properly is by adding an element that you would rather keep hidden from view. Hiding a purely functional element is not always easy, so consider making it a prominent, well-designed feature of the piece, something beautiful that will add to the design, rather than being simply a practical necessity.

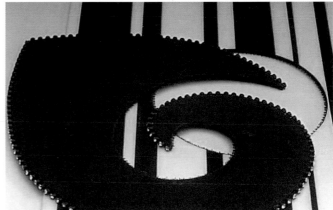

left The clean lines of this silver and acrylic brooch are enhanced by the simplicity of the steel pins. These double as a stand so that the form can be displayed as a miniature sculpture when not attached to the body.

above The function of this swirling piece is initially a conundrum – the flexible form allows it to be moulded by the wearer before it is secured to clothing or hair using Velcro.

function jeweller's showcase

"I am concerned with the relationship between wearer and object, and fascinated by the ways in which these objects can be worn, carried or experienced. I am motivated by simple mechanisms, and adapt new and unusual ways to open, close or attach a piece of work."

sarah may marshall

personal containers The minimal dome forms that are used to encapsulate and protect a precious 'seed', or pill, in these pieces, are reflections of natural seeds and pods, and colours from Trinidad, Sarah's place of birth. These were the inspirational starting points for her work. They were subsequently designed, then refined and developed through experiments in the designer's sketchbooks and workshop.

Each object has a story and a function to fulfil, so simplicity is of paramount importance in maintaining the clarity of the concept – the piece is carefully designed to avoid unnecessary distraction of complicated shapes and forms. The mechanism that allows the object to be worn and opened is conceived as an integral and vital part of the design, both on an aesthetic and a functional level.

opposite page The potential of an idea is explored through sketches and experiments, and is pushed further until it fulfils the function of the design. The piece titled 'Communication Accessory', (top) acts as a mood indicator. It contains coloured neoprene inserts that can be changed according to the wearer's disposition – blue to indicate calm, yellow to suggest warning, green to intimate envy and red to suggest sexuality. Below, the designer has experimented with other forms of containment.

left This gilded silver object with stainless steel mechanism can be carried in a bag as a pill box, or attached to the body as a piece of jewellery. The two domes open to release or contain a pill, such as a headache tablet, or other essential medication.

materials overview

Today there are no real taboos regarding materials in jewellery design. It is the appropriateness of a material and how it is treated that will add quality and value to a design and make it desirable, as can be seen in the transformation of humble materials such as plastic and paper, or ribbon and tin, for example.

traditional materials If asked which materials they most associate with jewellery-making, most people would name the 'noble' metals – silver, gold and platinum. There are historic reasons for this, as traditionally jewellery was a means both of investing wealth and displaying worth so that others could appreciate the financial status of the wearer.

There are also practical reasons for using gold and platinum: in their pure, unalloyed state they are inert metals – that is, they are chemically inactive and so do not oxidise or react to the body. This factor, combined with the value added because of their relative scarcity, makes them highly desirable for jewellery.

right The white bloom, achieved through pickling silver, contrasts with the gold which is used as detailing on the dense cluster of stems of this ring.

left These two rings have been deftly crafted to look like ribbon. One is made of palladium – a metal that is rarely seen in jewellery – and the other is gold, a more traditional and obvious choice.

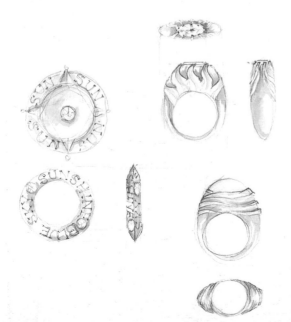

left and above Pearls and diamonds, and gold and diamonds are used to depict the moon and the sun respectively. In one set of designs lettering (SUN, SUNSHINE, BLUE SKY and MOON) is used as a means of explaining the concept, while in the other the materials are used as a more subtle indicator.

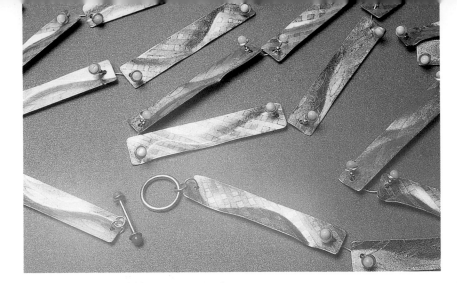

For those who could not afford gold, there was silver, sufficiently scarce to be prestigious, but less so than gold. Although silver does oxidise, it does not react with the body excessively, and can be worn by most people.

Pure gold and silver are in general too soft for jewellery making; they are ductile, malleable metals and lose their form too readily, so both are usually alloyed (mixed with other metals) to make them workable.

above Tin plate, a material not normally associated with jewellery, is used to make chain links that have been coupled with precious platinum and gold leaf in various shades.

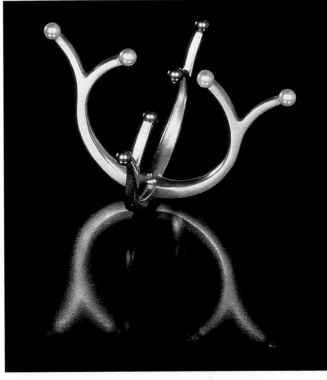

natural and symbolic materials
Natural materials have been used throughout the centuries, for decoration or to introduce colour to metal pieces. In ancient cultures, some materials were also valued for their symbolic connotations – for example, in traditional Chinese culture pearls, said to be the tears of dragons, are associated with sorrow, and jade is considered lucky because it warms to the human body and is thought to be capable of projecting the luck of the wearer.

Often the symbolic meaning of a material is related to strength or vulnerability of that material. Opals, for example, are considered unlucky, which is due to the fact that they have a high water content and so can be tricky to set – if set in a loose collet in warm weather they might shrink and fall out in cool weather.

Other natural materials, such as crystals, are believed to have inherent qualities that may aid healing and promote spirituality. Knowing what a material symbolises can help to make your design intentions clearer.

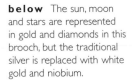

below The sun, moon and stars are represented in gold and diamonds in this brooch, but the traditional silver is replaced with white gold and niobium.

above Although the gold and pearls used in this marvellous ring are traditional materials, the form is clearly contemporary. The design's modernity helps to rejuvenate the conventional materials, while also ensuring that the piece retains desirability.

materials case studies

Silver detail around the eye and mouth punctuates the visual impact.

Using painted paper allows the designer to play with colours. Here the bold primary colours are merged to soften the effect and add visual interest.

left Silver was used to back up a set of colorful paper pins, not only physically but also psychologically—silver is thought of as being precious, so the relative value of each of these pins is increased by its inclusion.

below A fringe of fine red ribbon introduces color, texture, and movement to this bangle. The bold base is fabricated from silver.

Materials are often pigeon-holed, and this has its pros and cons. It is useful for a designer to use the conventional image of a material to represent an idea, and it is also advantageous to revisit that image to push the boundaries and enliven jewellery design.

combining silver with alternative materials

Combining traditional and alternative materials can add useful contrast to a design that allows it to maintain the familiarity of a traditional jewellery material while having a contemporary edge. Silver is a traditional material that lends itself particularly well to this end; as it has a neutral colour, it can easily be combined with other materials that can be brought to a piece specifically to add colour.

On the set of pins (above), silver is used more as a neutral structural element onto which paper can be attached. A glimpse of the silver surrounds the eyes and the silver base can be seen from the back. The fact that the piece does incorporate a precious metal like silver, also ensures that it is taken more seriously as a 'real' piece of jewellery than it might be if it was made of coloured paper alone.

right The shape and scale of the egg form give a clue as to the type of shell that is embedded in the ring – quail.

The silver base adds intrinsic value, as well as structural strength.

The embedded shell fragments create a speckled effect, cleverly mimicking the surface of a real egg.

left Agate is a semi-precious stone that is challenging to work with because to do so requires specialist tools and skills. It is not generally thought of as valuable, but its beauty and value are enhanced by craftsmanship and design.

right This bangle is a clever play on materials; it appears to be made of wood – and in some ways it could be said that it is, since it is constructed of sheets of layered paper, which at first glance resemble wood grain.

The inspiration behind the ring (opposite page, bottom) is quite obvious. Not only is it shaped like a quail egg, but eggshell has actually been mixed with silver and resin to form the material. The shell brings colour to the design and helps to confirm the design concept.

On a bangle that demands attention (opposite page, centre), ribbon has been combined with silver, bringing contrasts in colour, texture and form to the design. Because ribbon is inexpensive, it can also be used in quantity, making for a greater visual impact. Any material that is appropriate to the concept is fitting for jewellery.

value adding Many designers do not restrict themselves to precious materials, instead they try to consider how to transform non-precious materials so that the perceived value is increased. By working with these materials they can challenge public preconceptions while also stretching their design skill.

This designer of the paper neckpiece and bangle has chosen to use a material that is not immediately associated with jewellery, namely paper, to create a very individual look. She has considered how paper can be transformed into a format that is appropriate for the design intention and also durable enough for the general purpose of the piece. This can be a very useful way of working, as designs made of materials that are not commonly used in jewellery are more likely to stand out from the crowd.

below Paper cord is hand-dyed and knotted to make an elaborate neckpiece. With sensitive handling and good design the most humble of materials can be transformed.

Craftsmanship can also be used to raise the perceived value of a material. As can be seen in the agate bangle (above left), the simplest of materials can be made to feel precious if the workmanship has sensitivity and quality. However, not all materials are easily worked, and some, such as stone, will require specialist skills and tools. To make the agate bangle, a designer would have to have at least a basic understanding of specialist lapidary, otherwise they could not be absolutely sure that such a design was achievable. If a designer does not understand how a material can be worked, they risk creating designs that are inappropriate and cannot be realised.

materials jeweller's showcase

" I take the materials I have at hand, combine them to find suitable alloys (technically and aesthetically), and proceed to transform them and blend them, adding and taking elements according to the feelings the materials themselves elicit from me. "

manuel vilhena

'it's upside down, back to front!' These rings were inspired by the recurring problem of how to place photographic transparency slides in the viewing tray of a projector, and by the raw power of the materials. Handmade from silver and moonstone, the rings are in themselves carriers of implicit meanings, and the materials are fascinating for the possibility of expression they possess. It is the designer's intention that these subtle, and sometimes hidden, possibilities are expressed in the work.

For Manuel Vilhena, jewellery is like cooking: it is a matter of taking the ingredients and combining them to get the best result. This involves the question of proportions, the correction of tastes, the final aesthetics of presentation, colour and fragrances, and above all, remembering that the finished product is to be 'consumed'. Making is a means of expression, and – just as the poet uses letters and words and the chef uses food and spices – silver, gold, wood and alloys are potential ingredients for the jeweller.

opposite page In these neckpieces, made from a variety of materials including wood, silver, and a special alloy of silver and copper called 'shakudo', there is no conscious attempt to forward opinions or views on a certain subject or material – although, from the standpoint of the viewer, these might be present. The wearer/viewer, in the absence of a plausible explanation, will automatically start to formulate one of their own.

right In these identical rings the stones are set in a pleasing composition that reflects a love of aesthetics and the act of actually making jewellery. The pieces are created as structures that can be shown upside down over a mirror that exposes their interiors.

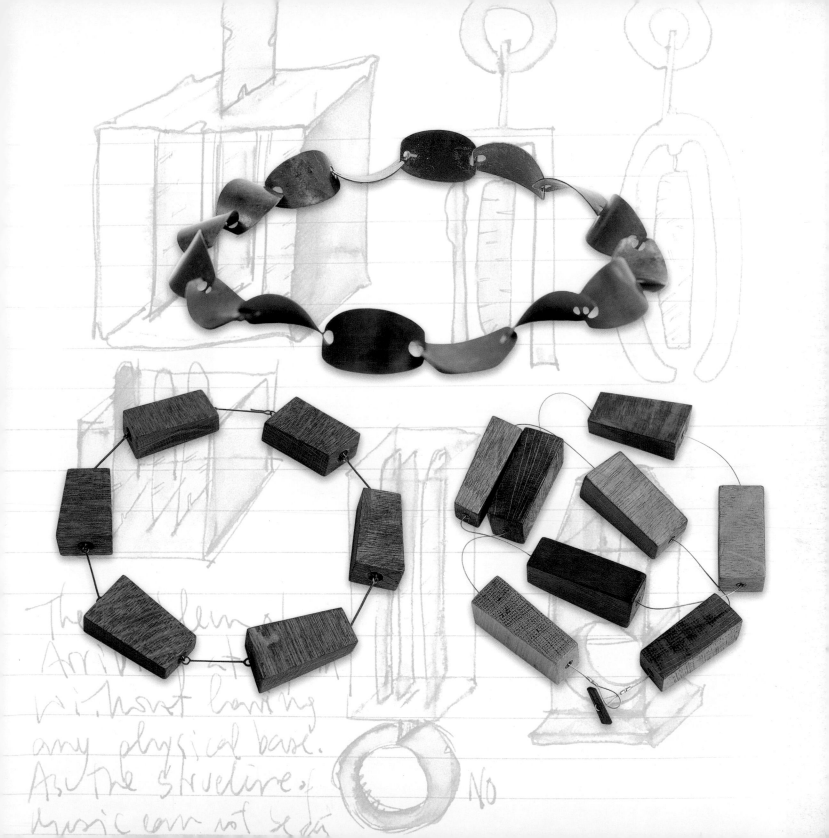

processes overview

The processes available to jewellers today are as varied as the materials used, and the possibilities open to a designer are limited only by the designer's own imagination and know-how. However, this kind of choice can make it difficult to decide which process to specialise in, as a jeweller can by no means master all.

knowing the facts The complexity of some processes can make them unsuitable unless you have an in-depth knowledge of the particular techniques, so designing to include them may not be straightforward. You may need to spend some time researching processes either by reading up about them in good technical manuals, or learning about them in a workshop environment. Some processes, such as mokumé gane for example, may be more difficult to access, as they require specialist machinery or materials that are not commonly found. You will need to try and gain access to them through the relevant expert, or a suitably equipped specialist educational establishment.

right The ancient art of lacquerwork is coupled with simple, modern jewellery forms, and the happy outcome is refreshing-looking jewellery and a new lease of life for the technique.

below Brass wire is used to make sample patterns and forms. The resulting models allow a designer to assess the design potential of the sample, as well as provide an opportunity to push the boundaries of the process.

signature techniques To refine basic jewellery skills so that a well-crafted piece of jewellery can be realised is challenge enough, so as a designer-maker the most productive course may be to concentrate on a technique that really inspires you and motivates you to keep on making and designing. Focusing on perfecting and exploring a specific sphere of activity can help you to establish a distinctive design style, and also a reputation for skillful handling of a particular process.

left Here, knitting is used as a means of defining three-dimensional form. The combination of knitted silver and rubber cord gives the design a quirky feel, while the ambiguity of the form invites the imagination to suggest what it represents.

Some designers become master craftspeople of a particular process by developing a technique in a pioneering and unique way. Whether you choose to design and master techniques whose sheer complexity prohibits others from following suit, or alternatively, take an easier path and use simple, existing techniques in an original way, the overriding concern must be to make the process part of the whole concept. With good design and an open and inquiring attitude, you can be innovative and inventive with any technique. Exploring new avenues in whichever process you choose to master can be a means of establishing your style and name as a designer-maker who specialises and excels in the application of that process, thereby making it a signature technique.

right Modern explorations in bonding techniques have revolutionised the metals that can be used to make technical advances in the ancient Japanese art of mokumé gane. Some of the combinations of metals in these three brooches are unique, and have never been achieved before.

processes case studies

Through a modern innovative approach to process, fresh and exciting possibilities can be brought to jewellery design.

old and new The fabrication of these earrings involves the traditional techniques of leafing and pressing, and traditional materials – platinum and gold leaf. However, these materials and processes are handled in combination with a considerably less traditional material for jewellery making – tinplate – making the work more unusual and interesting.

The traditional processes have also been used in an innovative manner. Pressing is often used to create forms, but is less frequently used to create blanket textures. Inspired by textiles and the observation of fabric folds, the designer has used the pressing process to create undulating surfaces in the tinplate. The patterns, likewise, were developed from investigations into colour and stitching in textiles.

By using the hand-worked process of leafing, production and material costs are kept to a minimum, allowing this designer-maker to be in complete control of the pieces from conception through to realisation.

The sheets are pressed so the pattern and texture can be tested together.

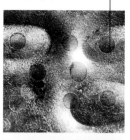
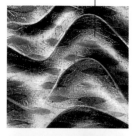

Light transforms the leaf-covered surface into a medley of highlights and lowlights.

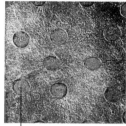

Flat samples are made of tinplate so that the pattern alone can be tested.

above Tinplate samples trial patterns and textures to create the look of fabric.

below Simple stud earrings are made from humble tinplate. The studs can be made to echo the pattern on the tinplate to give a sense of continuity.

key points

How processes are used and combined can help to determine a designer's individual style

✳

Making exploratory samples and models can help achieve unexpected and exciting results

✳

Collating material and test results in a technical journal enables repetition and development of process

creative colour A lot of design work is done on paper, but it is important to experiment with the actual components and models before finalising a design. The items pictured here represent trials made for a series, the final pieces of which were fabricated from a combination of anodised and pressed aluminum, sand-cast pewter, coloured wire and plexiglas.

The designer has experimented with a variety of colouring and fabrication processes. Experiments with different dyes, pens, inks, etch resists and methods of layering coloured images of drawings, poems and words on anodised aluminum were developed so that the most luscious results could be achieved. Words and drawings were printed onto anodised aluminium sheets, which were then dyed various colours, and further coloured with pigment ink patterns. The colourful sheets were then pressed and cut to make components that could be used either on their own or combined with sand-cast pewter, acrylic and other collected objects

Anodising is an electrochemical process used for colouring certain types of metal and, with aluminium in particular, a wide spectrum of bright colours can be achieved. Jewellers with appropriate experience will sometimes anodise their own materials, but aluminium is anodised for industry and firms can be found that will colour pieces specially for jewellers.

right Copper and silver foil is pressed into etched sketches to test compositions that will be made in multimedia, including anodised aluminium.

below right Models made from cardboard cutouts, plastic-coated wire and laminate enable the designer to experiment with colour, print, drawing and layered effects.

below left Sheets of anodised aluminium are used to test different colour combinations and colouring processes.

Component cut from pressed and dyed aluminum.

Printed matter has been printed onto a flat, coloured sheet of aluminium, then combined with a drawn image of a dog.

Cutout from pre-coloured cardboard.

Plastic-coated wire.

An image is drawn freehand directly onto a coloured aluminium sheet with permanent markers.

Paper cutout, coloured in by hand with crayon.

Layers of colouring applied through different processes give the image visual depth.

processes jeweller's showcase

> My goal is to make objects not only optically playful or deliberately interactive, but also unconsciously enjoyable; I hope the work will be played with by the wearer without it being a deliberate action.
>
> **tomomi yokoyama**

kinetic rings These captivating ring forms were inspired by the geodesic domes of designer Buckminster Fuller. Tomomi Yokoyama began by making paper models of geometrically shaped rings with moving parts, to create a variety of impressions, ranging from the futuristic and the decorative, through to a sense of hardness and softness. The processes used to create three-dimensional forms in paper are the extension of her initial interest in the ancient art of origami, and by finding suitable mechanisms and solutions for working with harder materials, she was able to make a series of intricate silver rings.

As part of the process of design development, the designer considered applying different finishes to the surface of the metal in order to create the effect of optical play, and also developing the ring form further to incorporate a puzzle or to involve self-assembly, thereby involving the wearer in interactive play.

below and opposite page These fascinating structures present a variety of changeable forms that exploit kinetics in order to tempt the wearer to play with them. The designer uses the assembly of geometric shapes as a means of creating the idea of play, while the concept of change is expressed through movement. The process of making three-dimensional structures by using a variety of two-dimensional templates, has given rise to a variety of kinetic designs, including a link that can be made into a chain for bracelets or neckpieces.

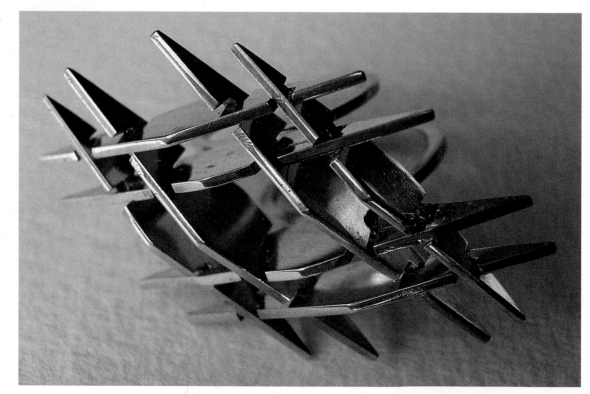

right The clean lines of the individual elements ensure that, once assembled, the design does not become too complex.

CHAPTER FOUR
CREATIVE CONCEPTS

Like so many things that are unfamiliar, the idea of a "concept" can appear rather daunting, but the word "concept" actually means nothing more frightening than "idea," and starting with a well-defined concept is fundamental to good design.

The following pages present some general themes that can form the foundation or basis of your concept. They are by no means definitive or exclusive, and as you design, some of the themes might merge and overlap. For example, you might find that the most effective way to express a narrative is through a piece that is also sculptural, while jewellery that symbolises a special event or occasion, such as an engagement or a wedding, will usually fit into the category of fine jewellery. All the pieces shown within these pages have further subtle ideas that flesh out the basic concept; these may be based on anything from love, to the passing of time, to social comment, and these are what distinguish each piece as unique.

There is nothing more thrilling than designing a piece of jewellery that actually works with your concept, and producing a piece that does exactly what you intended.

organic overview

The word 'organic' defines anything that is related to, or derived from, nature. In the context of jewellery design and fabrication, the term can refer to inspiration, materials, processes and design methodology, as well as aesthetics.

inspiration Nature has always been a popular source of inspiration, and holds so many unique forms to select from that we are spoiled with choices. Inspiration for practically every element of design can be found in nature, from shape, form, texture, colour and materials, through to function, emotion and processes. All of our senses can be satisfied by the organic world: visually stimulating forms and textures, tactile surfaces, unique sounds, arresting smells and delicious flavours. This world is a constant source that can be used to fuel design.

right The colour of these chrysanthemums is the first thing to attract attention, but each individual petal is also very sensual – the forms are a combination of delicacy and strength, making them a seductive source of inspiration.

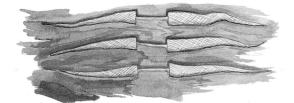

left This drawing of gently undulating pin forms is every bit as sensuous as the petals of a chrysanthemum that inspired the shapes.

left Here, a jeweller's inspirations are carefully housed; among the collection is an assortment of natural treasures, including a carved walnut, sharks' teeth, feathers, shells and fir cones.

right There is no mistaking the beautiful butterfly shapes and patterns that inspired this multi-functional silver pendant.

design 'Organic' can also describe a style of design development that imitates nature. Some designers prefer to allow a design to evolve as they work so that the result is more random and imitative of nature than it might be if it had been planned in a more structured and controlled way.

Perfectly straight lines, round forms or symmetrical shapes are not often found in the natural world, and are generally associated with the manmade. If a design is constructed from curvaceous, undulating lines, or if it is an abstraction from nature, such as a texture that imitates tree bark, then this also would be considered an organic design. Because so much of the material that is used in the design process has its roots in nature, there is a great deal of design that could be described as organic even if it is not overtly or obviously organic by the time the design is realised.

materials and processes The natural world is a rich source of materials for jewellery design and fabrication. Diamonds, the hardest natural material known to man, have long been familiar to us as a jewellery material. Over the years all kinds of other natural materials have been used, from feather and shell to teeth and hair.

While humankind's knowledge of the natural world is always expanding, we will never be able to control natural forces or predict their workings with absolute certainty. An organic process is one which, in the same way, involves an element of randomness, which means that the results cannot be precisely predicted. For instance, cold etching could be called organic because variables, such as tenacity of the etch resist, complexity of the design or strength and corrosive action of the etch solution, affect the outcome of the process. By contrast, photoetching is a fairly predictable, 'inorganic' form of etching, as the methods employed are mostly automated or mechanical, and the results can be planned with relative accuracy.

above This sensual piece is the embodiment of an underwater fantasy world where the iridescent colours of Atlantis are recreated as a witty acrylic ring that uses natural, organic forms.

right The design of this ring is distinctly organic, but less obvious is the fact that the materials – silver, aquamarine, and pearl – are also organic, as they too are derived from nature.

organic case studies

The wonder of nature is that ultimately it is the source from which everything comes, and to which everything will return. It is a timeless inspiration for artists and designers. It has strong symbolic potential, both on a personal and universal level, and can be appreciated purely for its intrinsic beauty.

relationships The designer of these brooches (top right) has used organic themes and materials to explore different kinds of relationships. The sketchbook pages (below) witness the development of ideas for a design based around the relationship between nature and a man, who is represented in the drawings simply as a face. The designer is not preoccupied with reproducing a close visual likeness to the natural objects – rather, it seems to be their symbolism that is important.

The two finished brooches are about love, growth and renewal. Sycamore seeds were collected by the dozen; a select few were cast in silver, and then combined with other symbolic shapes and materials. The immortalisation of organic forms through their inclusion in jewellery effectively arrests the inevitable process of decay. By casting the sycamore seeds in silver, the forms were preserved – at least for the life of the brooches.

Both designs relate directly to the organic inspiration, but do not aim to mimic nature. They capture elements of nature and transform them through a thorough design process into unique jewellery forms with a clear sense of symbolism and narrative.

paying homage to nature's beauty The designer of the brooch and bracelets on the opposite page is interested in the beauty of nature itself, rather than its potential for metaphor.

Fascinated by the boundless variety of textures, sculptural forms and constructional elements, the

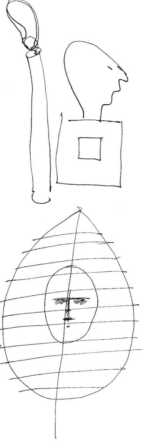

top right and right Ultimately, the interpretation of these brooches is left to the viewer – are the leaves symbolic of an idea, a place or, perhaps, people?

top left The simple sycamore seed coupled with a strong vertical form is enough to suggest a tree.

below left A rudimentary sketch combines a leaf with a face.

below The inclusion of easily understood symbols such as a love heart, which is also included in the final pieces, indicate this design sketch is about love and relationships.

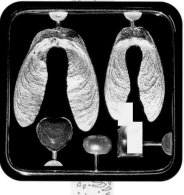

key points

A literal translation of natural forms into jewellery sets the challenge of achieving the perfection of the real thing

✳

Organic forms can be immortalised through processes such as casting and electroforming

designer has spent considerable time handling, examining and then drawing the leaves to develop a more intimate relationship with the forms and gain a better understanding of how they look and feel and move.

Her aim is to translate her vision of natural beauty into sculptural, wearable objects, so the quality of the leaves is directly referred to in an almost literal manner. This is not an easy task, as it means trying to emulate the perfection of the real thing.

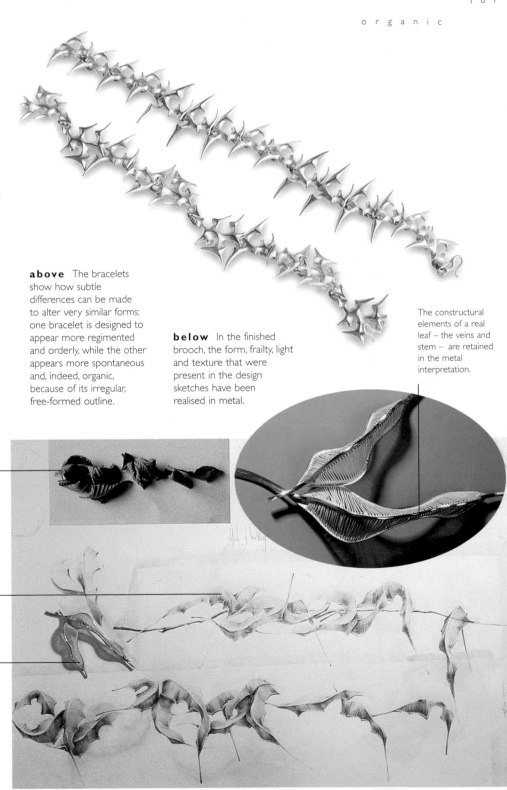

above The bracelets show how subtle differences can be made to alter very similar forms: one bracelet is designed to appear more regimented and orderly, while the other appears more spontaneous and, indeed, organic, because of its irregular, free-formed outline.

below In the finished brooch, the form, frailty, light and texture that were present in the design sketches have been realised in metal.

The constructural elements of a real leaf – the veins and stem – are retained in the metal interpretation.

The designer has included photographic imagery for visual reference.

Detailed drawings aim to capture form, texture, and movement.

Finally, the form is translated into metal.

above and right Delicate detailed drawings are used to explore organic forms and different ways of translating them into jewellery.

organic jeweller's showcase

" My work is based on organic themes, designed from drawings of seedpods, tendrils, pollen, shells and other natural forms. The pieces are often depicted in a state of decay, with necrotic or insect-eaten areas. The signs of decay are an expression of the beauty in death, a reaction to sanitised modern attitudes. " **paul wells**

tendril neckpiece The predominant themes in this work are connected with humankind's dominion over nature; it is also about capturing the preternatural feelings that can be invoked by natural forms and contemplation of nature as divine.

To keep the form's organic fluidity, its three-dimensional biomorphic form, and its strong surface qualities and tactility, attention to detail is very important. To give the piece flow, the pin and fixing mechanisms were made an integral feature of the design.

The metal techniques used to fabricate the pieces are ones that imitate or suggest natural forms and textures – rolling mill, striation, tapering, fold-forming, forging, punching, chasing and patination. The piece is constructed in silver because of the aesthetic qualities that can be achieved from the visual contrast between burnished white metal and oxidisation.

opposite page The elegant brooch (top left) manages to capture the hardness of a pod, designed by nature to protect the seeds within, and also its delicate frailty. The models are experiments in fold-forming, an organic, and therefore largely unpredictable, process, and the detailed background sketches not only replicate the shape and physical detail of the organic inspiration, but also capture mood and atmosphere. The drawings inform the work on many levels – they are important for assimilating details that help to make a piece of jewellery convincing; they provide information on how volume intersects with line or another volume, and how texture and pattern can help to describe volume and form.

left The chain and pendant undulate and flow as if they had, themselves, grown deep amongst the lush flora of an exotic Pacific jungle. The lightweight tendrils and pod invite handling, as the tactile forms suggest an intriguing, if mildly dangerous, haptic experience.

geometric overview

Based on mathematics, there is a sense of order and perfection about geometric forms that makes them useful shapes to contrast with other, more fluid elements of design. Framing a design in a geometric shape gives a useful, crisp neatness that can be embellished with ornament, yet not appear overworked.

in pursuit of perfection The very purity of geometric forms can be problematic: because we instinctively know, or imagine we know, how a geometric form should look, our eye expects perfection. We are therefore likely to notice any discrepancy in a geometric form, however minor, whereas the eye is more ready to make allowances if there is an inconsistency in a free-styled form. In the same way, a mistake in an organic shape could be seen as part of the character of the piece, while a mistake in a geometric form will almost certainly be read as a fault.

right The simplicity of the circular form prevents the surface texture of this striking bangle from appearing too fussy. There would be a danger of overkill if this busy pattern was used on a more complex form.

below left Concentric circles are carved, polished, textured and gold-leafed to create a brooch that transcends mere jewellery. The inherent beauty and calm of the piece suggest that another employment for the form could be as a focal point for meditation.

below This series of rings relies heavily on geometric form. Because the basic forms are so clean-cut, the detail is highlighted, making it more visually captivating. This means the detail can be appreciated as the focus of the design.

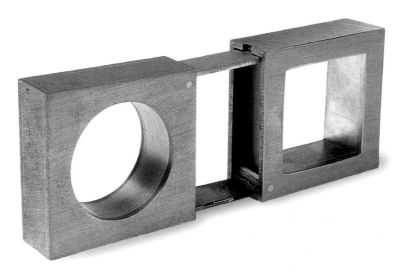

left The textural centrepieces in these arm-cum-neck-cum-ankle pieces, titled 'Sun and Moon', are appropriately set in simple geometric frames to ensure that the concept is not blatant or literal.

above Precision is crucial in this pair of geometric rings that interlock to become a double ring. Lifting the hinged lid on either form allows the rings to be joined as one. Yet, when apart the closed lids are almost undetectable.

below In this pair of handsome diamond rings the shape of the stone is echoed by the setting, which is made to be as simple and as clean as possible.

indicative of modernity Although geometric shapes have been with us since the beginning of time, making accurate, structured geometric forms is better suited to modern methods of fabrication than handwork is. Today, geometric forms can be made with such precision that they are almost clinical, suggesting modernity as opposed to antiquity.

Advances in technology have made high-precision machinery and equipment that lend themselves to accurate work. Contemporary Nordic designers tend to lean towards an incredibly precise way of working, while geometric forms made in the Americas can tend to be 'warmer' and less clinically precise. For some designers the challenge is to make handmade forms that are as perfect as machine-made ones; this results in a bizarre illusion, where the perceived value of craft and design are questioned and thus raised as a pertinent issue.

geometric jeweller's showcase

" For my "Millennium" piece I was naturally drawn to the subject of time, something that is preeminent in the public consciousness with the dawning of a new millennium — time, measured, precise, cyclical, constructed. "

elizabeth bone

'time signals 11' Time was the inspiration for this neckpiece, which was designed and made specially for a millennium exhibition. Elizabeth examined instruments to measure time, and also those factors that determine time — the sun, moon and stars. The growth rings of trees, shells and teeth were also sources of inspiration.

Materials and processes were guided by order, balance and modernist influences to form the basis for a work that is composed of clean lines and geometric forms. Although the piece was produced entirely by hand processes — sawing, filing, shaping and coaxing — the working vocabulary used contains many visual references to mechanical production.

The design process is exploratory: the designs developed through a matrix of maquettes where themes evolved and order emerged.

right References to metronomes and pendulums communicate the concept of time with sophistication and clarity. The precision of the form and the meticulous accuracy of the craftsmanship work in unison to produce a salient reversible neckpiece that celebrates the new millennium.

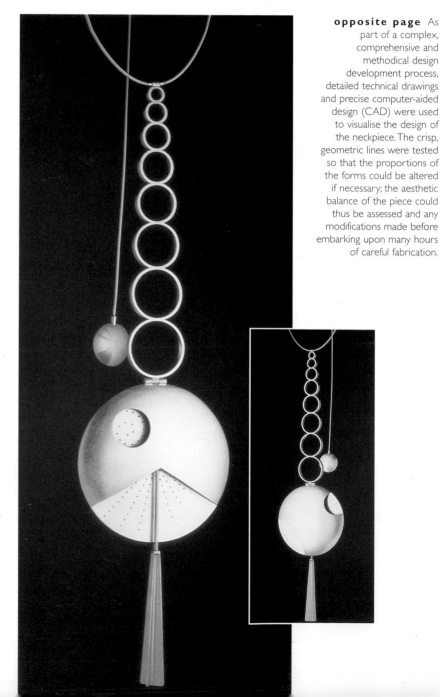

opposite page As part of a complex, comprehensive and methodical design development process, detailed technical drawings and precise computer-aided design (CAD) were used to visualise the design of the neckpiece. The crisp, geometric lines were tested so that the proportions of the forms could be altered if necessary; the aesthetic balance of the piece could thus be assessed and any modifications made before embarking upon many hours of careful fabrication.

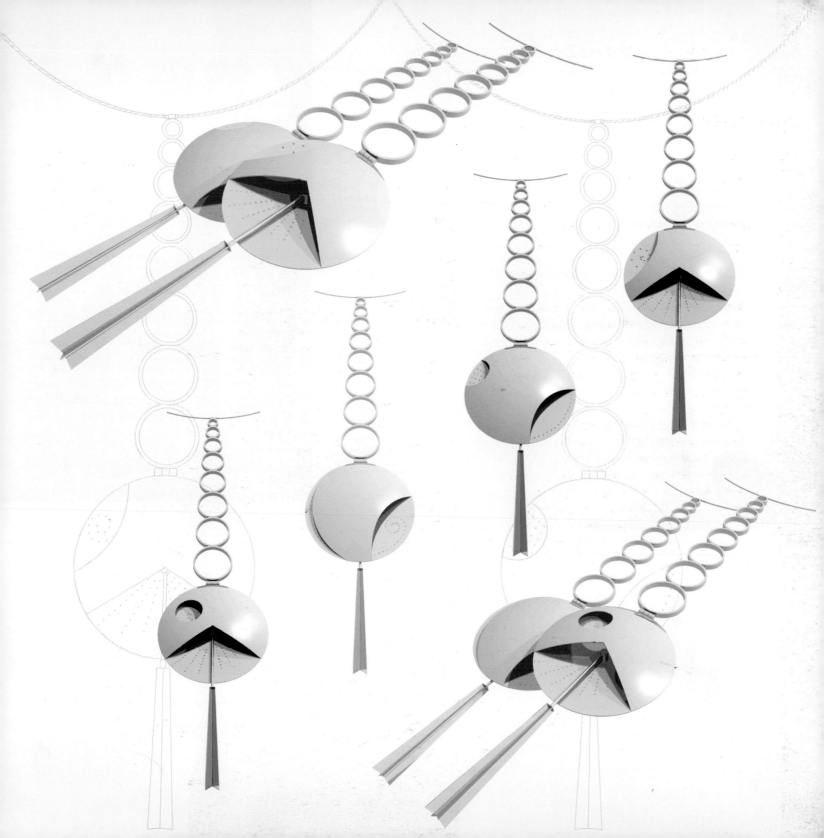

abstract overview

'To abstract' means 'to draw away, separate, remove or summarise, so that what remains is the essence of the original'.

obvious vs. subtle The word 'abstract' sometimes fills people with horror as they imagine stark minimalist art in which any resemblance to the inspiration has been obliterated. However, in much abstract art the original form or inspiration is still clearly recognisable; it has simply been cleansed so that it is less cluttered with unnecessary or peripheral detail.

Abstraction is a very useful design tool, and it could be said that the design development process should always involve abstraction in order to reduce peripheral information and enable the design to become more focused. The source of an abstracted shape, form or texture is developed during the design process so that it may be better suited to the concept, and so that it is better balanced visually and aesthetically. Through the process of abstraction the designer makes a comment on what he or she finds most interesting about an object,

right The form and texture of this ring are based on abstractions from organic forms. The translucent base of the ring is reminiscent of a jellyfish, and the form at the end of the extension is an attractive coral colour.

below In these books, design sketches and delicate montages of cell structures and insect wings were collated and explored as the inspiration for an abstract pattern. The structure of a skull and wing bone was then translated into Perspex to make a striking bangle form (pictured far right).

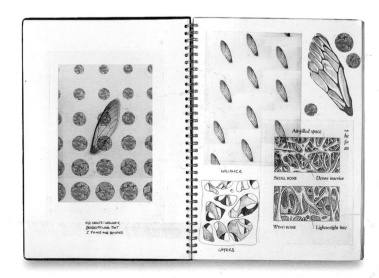

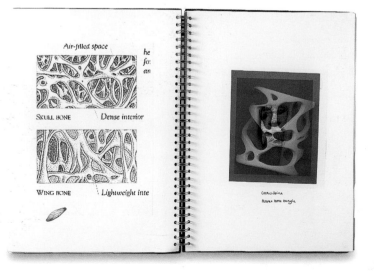

and the treatment of the materials is likely to tell the viewer something about the designer's viewpoint.

If the idea of abstracting seems confusing, try this simple exercise. Cut a 2.5cm (1 inch) square out of a piece of white paper and place this 'window' over an image in your sketchbook so that you cannot see the whole image. You are forced to focus on the exposed area. This is a simple means of abstraction at a very basic level, but it is a good place to start.

taking things literally

Abstracting is a useful way to avoid being too literal, which can cause designs to be predictable and dull. For example, if a fish were the inspiration for a piece, the obvious design would be to make a replica of the form of the fish. However, with a little more thought you might be able to make a more subtle, personal design statement. You might consider the colour of the scales and the flesh. Imagine a beautiful salmon, with its fine brown and grey-specked scales and radiant pink flesh. Imagine placing your 'window' over an area of the fish. This view could inspire you to think of enamelled detail – and there you have it, the beginning of a beautiful abstract jewellery design.

above Different patterns, including one abstracted from a zebra's stripes, have been superimposed onto the clean lines of an armpiece in a selection of models and templates.

above An upturned peridot was the inspiration for an uncomplicated silver ring that is an abstract bud form. The spiky details at the base of the bud act as grips so that the form can be turned to lower the stem of the bud, which has a seed at its end to change the size of the ring.

right This brooch form is an obvious abstraction of a spider and its web. Here, the design development process resulted in a mutually reliant form where spider and web are inextricably linked.

abstract case studies

The original scanned image shows all the details and texture of the fossil form.

Computer software is used to abstract texture.

The final image is completely cleansed of detail.

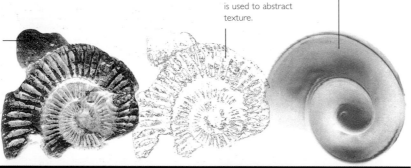

left The sweeping form of the sea fossil is simplified, cleansed of its texture and pulled into a more three-dimensional structure to make a repeatable unit that entertains the eye and invites one to run a finger along its smooth form.

right Unless you know your chemistry or botany, you might be left guessing about the inspiration behind these pieces. The crisp forms suggest a thorough research program in which precious samples were fastidiously collated. The final designs, based on abstractions from lemons, are modern, precise and visually appetising.

Abstraction is essentially about understanding and simplifying a subject so that its inherent quality can be given centre stage without any unnecessary distraction or competition.

nature and computers Computers can be a useful tool for jewellery designers, although acquiring the necessary technological skills can involve months of dedicated learning. The designer of the fossil pendants (above) scanned an image of a fossil into a computer, then abstracted it to the essence of its linear structure. The inspiration for the form is still evident in the finished pieces, but, by simplification and purification, the designer has added an element of sophistication that is not immediately evident in the source.

abstracting beauty Almost any form can be analysed and taken back to basics, and this is a useful process because it can offer a fresh look at a subject that might otherwise be taken for granted.

The designer of the three pendants (above right) chose the humble lemon as a subject, breaking it down and scrutinising it in order to represent its significant elements rather than the whole object. The acid of a lemon, the physical pith and an image of lemons called 'Buddha's Hand' are abstract components that become the decorative feature in no-nonsense silver frames. The sharp design suits the tart personality of the subject.

Unusual sources of inspiration, such as spiders (see opposite page), can result in interesting objects of beauty. By abstracting the attractive elements of the subject and making the pieces with materials that are tactile, such as metal and horn, the spider becomes a handsome rather than scary object. Framing an object of fear in a context that enhances its beauty, rather than positioning it in a composition that provokes horror, is clearly a helpful means of abstracting unpleasant stimuli that might affect the reception of a beautiful design.

key points

Modern technology can aid the process of abstraction

✳

Abstraction can enable a designer to locate beauty in an object that traditionally provokes fear or disgust

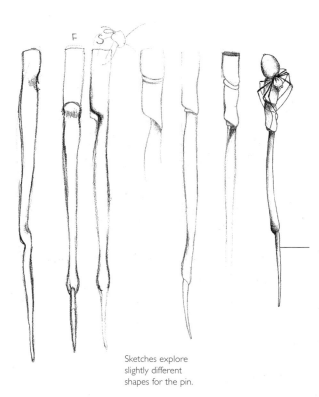

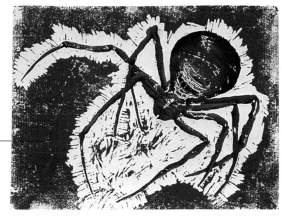

this page A spider was the inspiration for a pin that is obviously based on a natural form, but the form is not concerned with presenting an anatomically correct representation.

Photographs and drawings were translated into prints as part of the familiarisation process between designer and subject.

The final sketch in the series shows the finished design in more detail.

The spider form is the focal point of the design. However, although the design retains the beauty of the spider, it is an abstract rather than a literal interpretation.

Sketches explore slightly different shapes for the pin.

The delicate form of a spider was atmospherically lit and photographed for research.

The designer spent considerable time making models in horn before carving the final piece.

abstract jeweller's showcase

"My work is characterised by organic, sensuous, smooth, liquid forms that are constructed with highly textured surfaces. The colour of 18-carat yellow gold is used in juxtaposition with dark gray oxidised silver and matte silver to create a striking contrast."

catherine hills

'genesis' neckpiece Catherine's brief was to make a piece of jewellery for an exhibition celebrating the Millennium. She chose to make a very personal piece, as significant changes were taking place in her emotional life. 'Genesis' was inspired by the idea of the Millennium being the birth of a new era, and it celebrates the essence of creation.

The two connected and reversible elements represent the two sexes, with the male piece, in oxidised silver, balancing the brushed silver female form. When the chain is removed from the body it can be encased inside the male piece, and the female can rest against the male.

Designed as a theoretical rather than a practical piece, it is suggestive of a visual narrative through form, colour and texture. This actively encourages the viewer to use his or her own imagination to understand the associations suggested by the forms, which are abstractions of assorted objects and themes, including a heart, an apple, a woman's womb, and images of childbirth.

right The two forms are designed to have a strong relationship with each other, and are intended to fit together when not worn on the body. Because they are designed to be worn either way around, there is no conventional front or back to the pieces.

opposite page The designer began by embarking on an exploratory process that involved considerable visual research, including drawing the human anatomy, fruit, and animal forms, and collecting images of pregnancy and childbirth. Before finalising the piece, simple paper maquettes were used to help determine the exact size and proportions of the form. Tools were then made for fly-pressing the forms.

figurative overview

The human form has been well represented in art, and jewellery design is a discipline that continues this tradition.

body language The way we feel and react to our surroundings or to stimuli can often be read in our body language, and for many designers this can be the inspiration for figurative design. Understanding the human body is the most important factor in figurative jewellery-making, and many jewellers study life drawing to become more knowledgeable about the human form.

The experiences, places and people that touch our everyday lives can be interpreted through jewellery in the same way that they can be interpreted as a sketch, painting or piece of sculpture. The fact that jewellery is generally most effective in a three-dimensional form could mean that a certain amount of abstraction may have to take place to make a figurative design work well as a piece of jewellery.

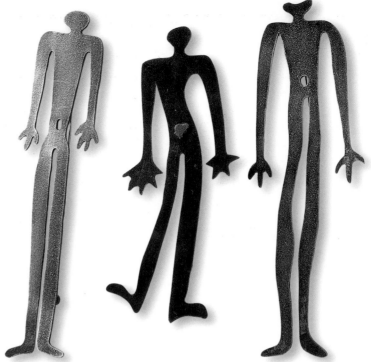

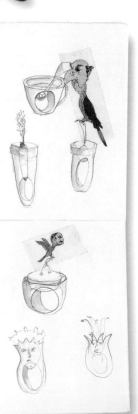

above Body language is astutely observed in this series of three brooches, where subtle inflections of the exaggerated limbs suggest the attitude, personality or state of mind of the each of the fanciful, abstracted figures.

left In this enigmatic brooch, titled 'Mask', the figures tell a story but the interpretation is left to the viewer: who is the figure with the mask? Who does the golden visage represent, and what is the relationship between the two?

right The figuratively absurd is explored in a number of quick sketches for ring forms.

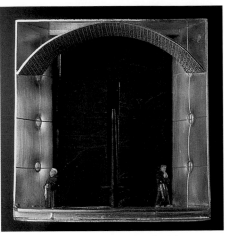

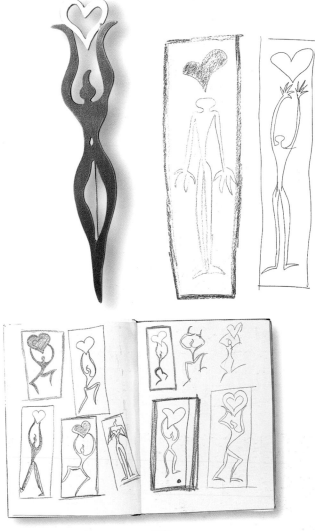

the human condition

The physical form is obviously fascinating in itself, but perhaps what is more interesting than form is the possibility of exploring the many associated aspects of the human condition through jewellery design.

Both human frailty and human strength are themes that have been explored and celebrated in art and literature throughout the ages. Every day we face challenges, defeats and triumphs, some of them big, many of them small, that can act as rich pickings for inspiration. Of course the range of individual human experience and emotion is limitless, but the human form is eminently recognisable and familiar to us all, and using it as a vehicle for self-expression can help make a designer's 'message' more accessible.

Figurative design is certainly not confined to serious statements or representations of humanity. Love and happiness, the absurd and the unfathomable all become inspirations for figurative work, and the human form is often used to express quite light-hearted and humourous ideas; it is an obvious means for poking fun at ourselves, as seen in caricatures that exaggerate the proportions or physique of a figure.

above These two brooches evoke the grandeur of Catholic churches; the scale of the portals suggests that this is no ordinary setting; and the dwarfed figures appear to be placed in a scene of great drama.

above right, centre, and below In a series of design development sketches a variety of poses describe the human condition. The symbols indicate the theme of each piece. The final piece, showing a female form, is evidently optimistic about love, the form being clearly both triumphant and celebratory.

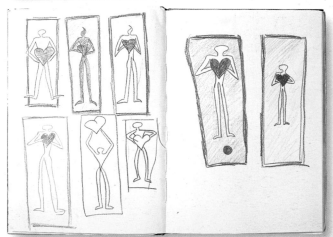

figurative jeweller's showcase

' My work has always revolved around thorough research into ideas, themes, and the material that I am exploring. My initial aim is to push techniques – both established and unknown or untested – and materials to their limits. '

yvonne kulagowski

'dancers' The inspiration for this piece is the human body – its structure, contours and the movements made through dance.

The properties of the material used, Perspex, also provided inspiration – its commercial colour range and ability to take on surface dye, its weight, its moulding and heat-forming possibilities and its ability to capture light through a sawn edge help to reproduce the energetic movement of dancers.

The figure is central to the piece, and life drawing was used to reinforce anatomical knowledge. A variety of media was employed, including charcoal and pastels for making quick, large sketches of dancers and their movements, and pen and ink for experimenting with the mechanics of the design. Extensive model making was carried out to ensure that the piece would be comfortable to wear and would also read as a collection of figures when not worn.

opposite page During the design development of this unusual earpiece, the body was carefully observed by making life drawings of the figure in exacting, confident and celebratory poses. Heated and pressed slivers of coloured Perspex are sandwiched between two thin sheets of clear Perspex, using similar colour combinations to those seen in Bakelite and Bandalasta. The hand-pierced Perspex pieces are then connected by sterling silver joints that were inspired by the articulated connecting elements used in the furniture industry.

above In this Perspex body piece, which looks like a chorus of dancers taking a bow, one repeated element reaches from shoulder to breast. The subtle colour emphasises the sawn edge and helps to draw attention to the additional colours in the detail area. The simple hooks allow the wearer the freedom to choose where and how the piece is worn.

narrative overview

Narrative work is generally engaging, as it offers the audience or wearer the opportunity to read a piece of jewellery that is designed to relate to an event or describe an action.

storytelling Because jewellery can combine painting and sculpture, or images and forms, in the one medium, it as an obvious vehicle for narrative.

Parallels can be made with the theatre. Like the theatre, jewellery provides a restricted space that can be dressed as a backdrop for a drama, comedy or thriller. Unlike a theatre, however, there are no live players, so narrative jewellery is a stage set for action. It may be up to the viewer to decide what the play will be and how it will end, or a particular ending might be implied. The 'stage' might merely present a tableau from which we are required to interpret the meaning for ourselves.

The characteristic small scale of jewellery generally requires the narrative to be told in a miniaturised format. This can heighten the associations with storytelling, the sense of mystery and wonder, as

below left How narrative work is packaged or exhibited can be a useful means of setting the scene so that the context of the narrative is more readily understood. This spider is part of a display for four rings that suggests a macabre world of secrets and intrigue.

right and below This glorious gold and enamel house breaks up into six pieces of jewellery. Separately the pieces tell of a bigger picture, and give insight into the working of the whole, which is hidden when assembled.

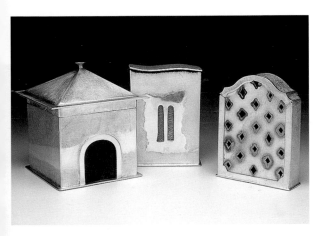

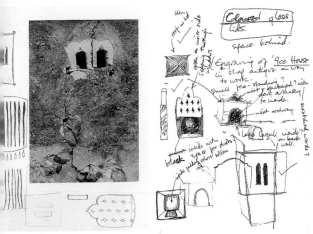

left, centre left Architecture seen on the designer's travels was the inspiration for this set of three forms. Two curious windows in a wall are as enigmatic in silver as they were in the bricks and stone of the original.

below left The corrugated roofs on these silver brooches suggest a warmer climate – but who are the characters waiting for?

below right Simple images made into silver pins are used to tell of the millstones of existence; a frail and beautiful butterfly bound to a range suggests woman's plight as a slave to domesticity, while the balloon is chained to the castle, unable to escape the apparent restrictions of a life of luxury.

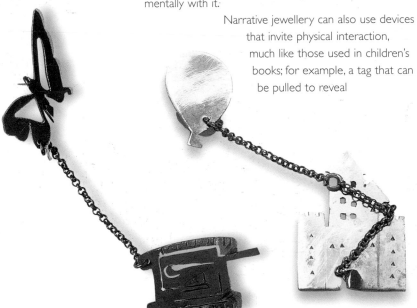

we are subconsciously taken back to childhood, to a time when our world was parallel, but miniature, to that of the giant adults around us.

interaction Storytelling is an interactive process, and narrative jewellery, designed to relate an event or describe a scenario, can include design devices to encourage interaction and invite the audience or wearer to 'read' the piece.

The viewer or wearer interacts with narrative jewellery by bringing their own imagination and interpretation to bear on the piece. For this to be possible, the basic idea needs to be mapped out, with essential information clearly 'setting the scene' – rather like a stage set – while additional or supporting material compounds the narrative. The title of the piece might be an important part of the stage-setting, or wording may be included on the actual jewellery itself to prompt further thought about what the piece is trying to communicate. Wording is effective on a number of levels. Firstly, the fact that it is there at all indicates that the piece is trying to 'tell' us something, and in the process of reading, we are encouraged to engage mentally with it.

Narrative jewellery can also use devices that invite physical interaction, much like those used in children's books; for example, a tag that can be pulled to reveal

narrative jeweller's showcase

> Whether physically or cognitively, every minute of every day we make a journey through time and space – "Crossing" is a *memento mori*, a commemorative piece that tells of the journey made by a family member into the afterlife.
>
> **jack cunningham**

'crossing' Making jewellery is a way to capture encapsulate, and ponder feelings and emotions. Through honing and constructing the brooch form repeatedly, Jack Cunningham explored and refined a means of expressing the fragments of life as narrative pieces that act as a snapshot from a diary.

Using a variety of shapes, symbols and materials, the brooches explore a catalogue of memories, experiences, sensations and encounters. In this beautiful and melancholic piece, the deeply felt loss of a family member is remembered and recorded. The winged cross suggests an angel, while the ruler indicates the lifespan of the loved one who is the subject of the piece.

opposite page In the sketchbook images, forms and symbols are combined to experiment with compositions that are narratives of life experiences, sensations and encounters. The importance of people, and how their presence or absence impacts the designer, is clearly significant. Caricatures of human faces feature in various enigmatic compositions that often offer glimpses of the context in which a drama may be placed, while still requiring the viewer to make their own judgements about the forms and symbols that act as prompts for the imagination.

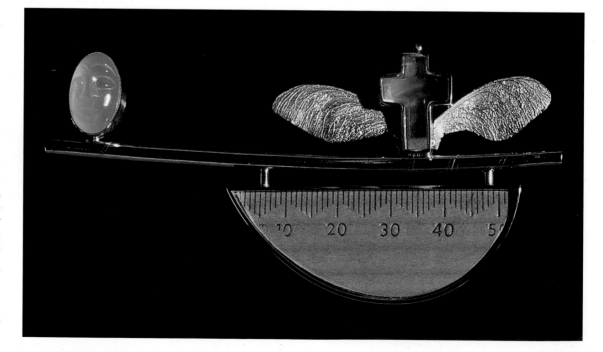

right This brooch speaks of a life cut short and the immense weight of loss for those who mourn, but at the same time, it is uplifting and optimistic – the winged cross suggests a journey to a superior existence, and affirms that faith and hope will sustain those who are left to remember the passing.

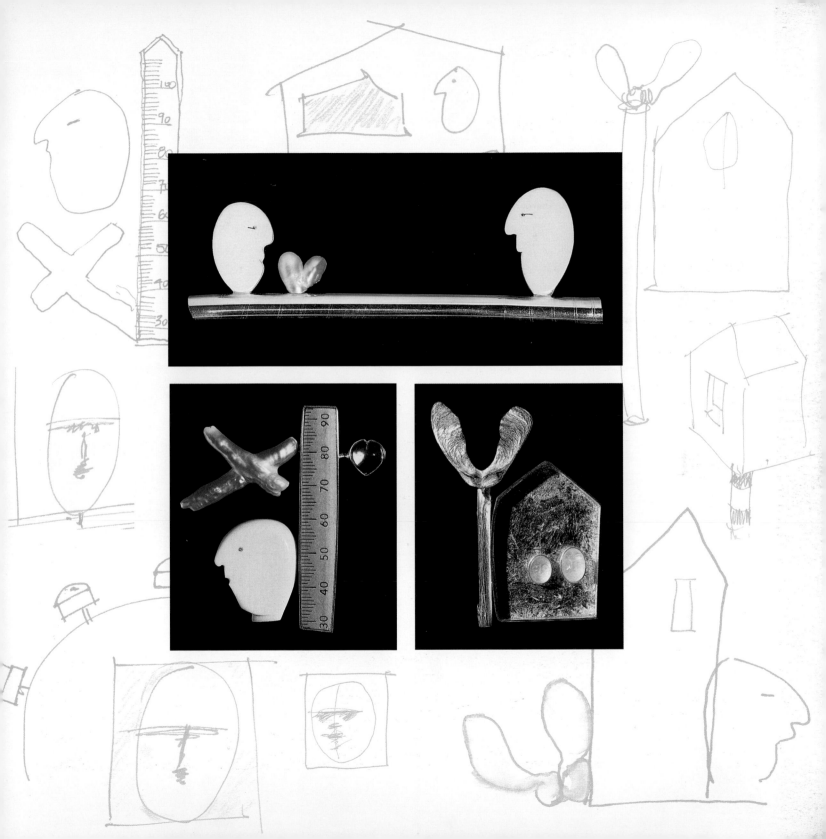

symbolic overview

Jewellery can be symbolic in a number of ways. It can symbolise a union, promise or pledge, or commemorate a special event; or it may be that the devices and materials included in the design have symbolic associations that advance the concept and design intention.

commemorative symbols Certain forms of jewellery have great symbolic significance, and the emotions that they inspire are based on learned responses to their traditional symbolism rather than their actual design. A simple wedding band, for example, is one of the most universally understood images, telling of a union between two people, regardless of their creed or culture.

Designers often need to consider the symbolic nature of a piece, because some events have recognised jewellery forms associated with them – in America, graduation from high school or university is often marked by a graduation (or class) ring – much like

above This series of rings includes materials that might not be to everyone's liking, yet there is something deliciously macabre about the tiny teeth that makes one question who they belonged to before they became jewellery objects.

left Human hair is captured behind rock crystal in a pair of wing-shaped 22-ct gold earrings with pearl details. The texture of the forms does much to integrate the hair into the pieces so that it does not appear obtrusive.

a signet ring – that is specific to the institution where the studies were completed. A special event will often be marked by the commissioning of a piece that includes certain significant elements that have special symbolic meaning for the individual or group making and receiving the commission.

superstition and religion

Certain materials and forms have symbolic meaning based in superstition or religious belief. For believers, both are likely to be highly emotive, and these objects are often said to have real power; they are treated with immense reverence by the initiated, and gain increased preciousness because they are venerated objects.

Amulets that ward off evil are frequently worn as jewellery, and as such it is believed that to be most effective they should be worn constantly, preferably close to the body. Talismans likewise are objects made of symbolically potent materials – they are thought to

right and below The meaning of this brooch, titled 'Love Kit', is open for the viewer to interpret. Juxtaposed next to an image that inspired the form, the viewer might think of the 'Love Kit' as being representative of who and what is entombed. Perhaps these forms are symbolic of the prerequisites for eternal bliss on the 'other side'.

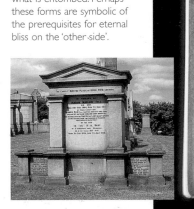

left The traditional unbroken round form of a wedding band has been abandoned for a signet shape in this piece. The inclusion of a pertinent symbol has been used as an emblem to mark the marriage. Although the rings are nonconformist, the design has great meaning for the wearers, and has as much importance for them as the traditional wedding band.

have magical powers that protect and bring good fortune, and are often seen in jewellery form.

Because there are many forms and materials that are thought to have mysterious power, it is useful, in design terms, to consider how these are perceived and how they may be used as a means of expressing your concept – for example, a four-leaf clover is thought of as lucky, while a downturned horseshoe is considered unlucky.

For some people, finding that human hair or teeth had been included in a piece of jewellery would make them very uncomfortable. However, these relics have enormous power and, used with care, they can also make potent design statements.

Most materials and shapes have symbolic meaning that can be used to help communicate design intention

✳

Using symbols that have more than one meaning can create a double entendre and introduce humour or useful ambiguity to a piece

symbolic case studies

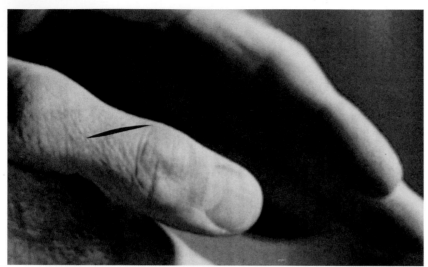

left and above
The dramatic image of a hand with a blood-red slash was the inspiration for the concept of this silver ring. With its dynamic cut, the design is so simple that it looks like it could become a second skin.

Everyday objects or events can often become symbolic of something more significant to particular individuals. Jewellery can be designed to acknowledge these symbolic links in order to create items that are representative of an event, emotion or idea.

right 'Paving slab-meets-jewellery' in this no-nonsense silver form set with concrete. The designer has inscribed marks in the top face of the ring.

marks and scars It is the urge to 'make our mark' that tempts us to leave a footprint in wet concrete. Such marks can therefore be a symbol of permanence. This symbolism could be combined with others – for example, instead of an engagement ring, a couple could commission a piece where they can sign their names in concrete.

The pieces on this page reflect the designer's interest in marks as symbols of an event or emotional experience. Physical scars were a source of inspiration that evolved into a simple design in which the scar is a metaphor for all the injuries, both physical and emotional, that we all carry. They become symbolic of an experience, borne of a single significant instance in our lives.

metaphors for life Symbols of the journey through life provide inspiration for many designers. The piece on the opposite page symbolises the protection of a home environment. The box represents a nest and contains a ring that is symbolic of growth; the growth of the seedling represents a thirst for knowledge. If the ring is worn, it risks damage; if left in the box, it is safe but hardly visible, symbolic of our potential frailty outside the protection of the home environment.

A series of ring forms are considered, including a bird, tree, seed and egg, in order to ascertain which is the most appropriate.

Paper templates were used to test the form and proportions of the box.

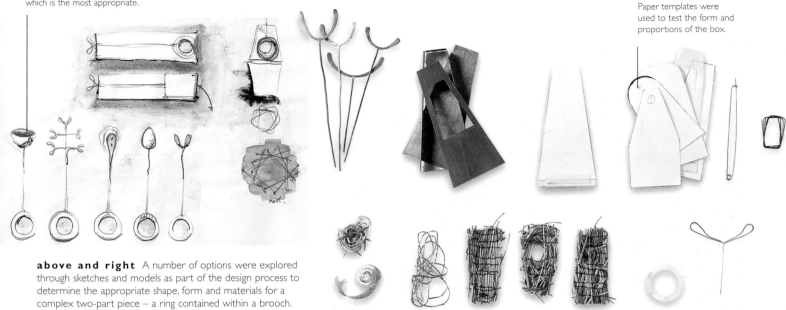

above and right A number of options were explored through sketches and models as part of the design process to determine the appropriate shape, form and materials for a complex two-part piece – a ring contained within a brooch.

The shape of the box form is also significant; it is reminiscent of a coffin or a metronome, a symbol of the passage of time. The piece is made predominantly of steel, which is seen as a strong, heavy material. For this design, thin sheet steel has been used so that the finished piece is remarkably light. Its delicacy helps to reduce the danger of the box appearing too overwhelming or oppressive.

The physical handling of the piece is integral to its concept; only by exploration and handling of the form can the viewer gain knowledge about the piece and discover what hides inside.

right The box and sapling are used as metaphors for life experiences – only part of the ring may be viewed while the box is closed, just as only part of a person's potential is seen within the confines of the home.

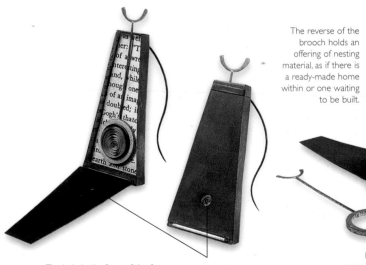

The reverse of the brooch holds an offering of nesting material, as if there is a ready-made home within or one waiting to be built.

The hole in the front of the form represents the entrance to a bird box, serving as a temptation to the viewer and as a link with the outside world for the seedling. The text inside is an analytical essay on the subject of nests.

Everything has its purpose – the brooch pins are designed so that the piece need not be worn, and serve both as a clasp and a stand for this miniature sculpture.

symbolic jeweller's showcase

❛ My symbolic commemorative jewellery is inspired by the connection between my clients and the important events in their lives. The inception of the work was, for me, very personal — six years ago, my youngest brother was killed in an accident, and his loss had a profound influence on my life. ❜

whitney abrams

opposite page The necklace, earrings and ring form part of the designer's collection of commemorative work. The gemstones and other elements used in the pieces, such as hair, flowers, photos and other representations of the individual, are symbolic of people or experiences. Capturing a memory, honouring an individual and celebrating occasions in life with these unique symbols can provide a great form of strength and expression for the wearer.

mourning flip ring Jewellery offers a means of expressing feelings of grief and bereavement, and Whitney Abrams chose to honour the memory of her brother with a special piece that incorporated locks of his hair. This was a cathartic experience that opened up to the designer the power of symbolism in healing and the importance of commemorating one's experiences in life, both happy and sad.

The understanding of mourning jewellery in Victorian times had a large influence on the designer's commemorative work, and the addition of gemstones and crystals to the pieces focused on more than just the aesthetic; they brought various symbolic meanings to the work. Healing, Zodiac associations, and personal connections were just a few of the additional dimensions provided by the gemstones. Seeing the importance these amulets brought to people's lives encouraged the designer to broaden the parameters of her work to encompass celebrations of birth and other important events.

right Hair is captured between a carnelian intaglio and rock crystal in this poignant gold ring that is a personal reminder of a loved one. The central section of the ring can be flipped so that the wearer has the choice to share the purpose of the piece, or keep its significance hidden and private.

icons overview

Icons are shorthand images or pictographic representations that may be used like a badge to summarise an ideology, describe a terrain, epitomise a subject or draw attention to a hazard.

enduring and evocative An icon or symbol is a means of associating a design with a particular issue or subject. Icons are often linked to issues that were pertinent at the time the icons were produced, such as nuclear disarmament, and they may also be culture-specific, such as the Statue of Liberty.

Many icons and symbols are recognised globally, while others may be specific to a smaller body of people. The love heart, for example, has been used for centuries and is an enduring motif that is readily understood by all. Other icons, such as the yin-yang symbol, have been around for as long but have only recently become universally recognised.

above A pair of bracelets with symbols pierced in plain and lightly textured silver buckles. The symbols provide the decorative element as well as the vehicle for the concept. The result is clean, clear and eminently wearable.

top right A love heart frames a house motif, suggesting that the designer is exploring the symbiotic relationship that might exist between these two elements of life.

right A heart sits innocently in the middle of a pendant form surrounded by a poem that speaks ambiguously about love.

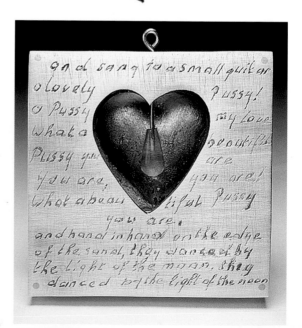

religious icons Jewellery has long been associated with faith. Many religions have an icon that typifies their creed – the cross in Christianity, the Star of David in Judaism and the crescent in Islam, to name but a few, are enduring icons that are seen regularly in jewellery.

Icons and symbols, particularly religious ones, can provoke great emotion and evoke automatic responses, so it is important that you take the time to research and understand the icon that you intend using in your design. Some may not translate well across cultures. The swastika, for example, is remarkably similar to a symbol used in Buddhism, except that it is a mirror image. This unhappy coincidence may be useful for a design that intends to make a specific comment or is based around a double entendre, but it may also be a minefield of misunderstanding.

left The addition of blood-red heart motifs around the bezel transforms this piece from a simple ring into a token of love. The sentimental splendour of the piece tempts us to conjure up a suitable love story.

right Potent Christian icons include the cross and the thorns of the innocent-looking rose, which are connected with the image of Christ wearing a crown of thorns.

left A page from a designer's sketchbook examining the purpose and identity of different icons in a collection that evokes various aspects of life.

key notes

A single icon may
have a myriad of
meanings
or associations

✳

The strength or impact
of an icon can be
increased or diminished
according to how it
is treated

icons case studies

By a process of brainstorming, you should be able to
look at an icon, motif or symbol and see how it can
change its meaning when placed in different contexts.

religious icon to medical alert The
cross has many meanings in addition to its religious
symbolism. It acts as a marker ('X marks the spot')
or can indicate 'No' on a form. On a math test, it
might mean that the answer to a question is wrong,
and elsewhere on the same test it might indicate the
multiplication of two numbers. A cross can be seen
as a kiss, a mark on a ballot paper or an indication
that medical assistance is close at hand.

The iconic cross is a recurring theme for the
designer of these brooches (below), who interprets

below The designer is
clearly fascinated by the
cross form and has recorded
many different examples
as inspiration.

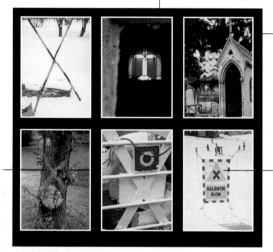

In a religious context,
a cross is shown in a
glimpse of stained glass.

Again the
cross is seen
in a religious
context, but
here there is
a stronger
emphasis on
death.

'X' marks the spot. It
might indicate that
the tree is to be
chopped down or
plot a point on a
navigation course.

'X' indicates
a warning.

below In this series of
brooches, the cross form is
represented in three
different ways. The viewer is
thus invited to draw his or
her own conclusions about
the meaning and significance
of the use of the cross.

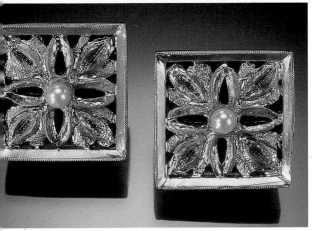

left A gold cross form is the basis for a resplendent centrepiece in a traditional pearl choker.

above Diluting its meaning does not weaken the appeal of the cross as a form. The symmetry and equality of these earrings make them neat, orderly, strong, and visually satisfying.

it in a variety of ways, thereby inviting the viewer to bring his or her own ideas to the piece.

For the designer of the earrings and neckpiece (above), the cross motif has been used as a decorative element – although it may still have symbolic connotations for both the designer and the viewer, even if they are only subconscious. The designer is aware of the strength of association of the iconic cross form, but has designed the framing and embellishment to diminish its symbolic impact. The combination of the rich, gold cross forms with precious pearls also gives the designs a retrospective feel.

set me free Fish have long been a symbol for spirituality and wisdom. The piece below, entitled 'Don't Box Me In', is designed as a riddle for the wearer or viewer. Only by handling the piece does the solution become clear – the form comes apart so that the fish can be worn to adorn one ear, while the box decorates the other. The earrings are designed to be a light-hearted conundrum, where the eventual outcome is freedom for the fish. Cuttlefish casting was used to create the surface texture that captures both the sense of scaliness and the movement of a fish.

left and below A simple drawing is made to visualise the design and check the aesthetics before the fabrication of a puzzling form that looks more like a trophy than a pair of earrings. The finished piece is simple, bold, and yet delicate, but only the simplest techniques were utilised in its fabrication.

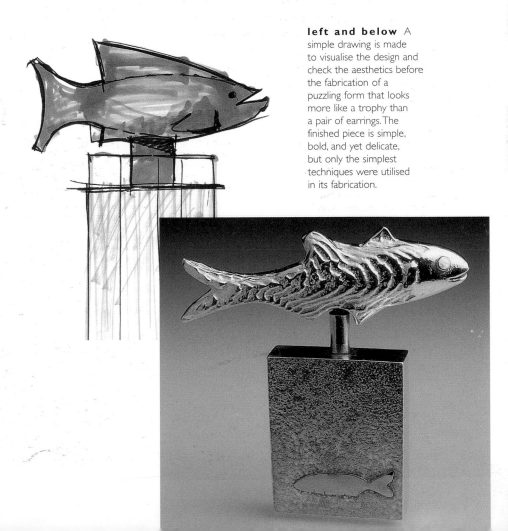

icons jeweller's showcase

‘ This reveals a somewhat acerbic view of designer-label devotees. The collection gently mocks those people who hardly bother to remove the price tags from their clothing in the rush to flaunt their latest purchases, and who revel in the conspicuous consumption that their wealth permits. ’

stacey lorinczi

'heartsick for America' This neckpiece, in old costume or sentimental jewellery style, was inspired by Marc Jacobs' classic, slightly camp, subversive, and coy aesthetic. The chain, made of arrows, has a price tag attached to it in a reference to consumerism, although the main focus is clearly the gun/heart combination. The serious problem of American gun culture and the preponderance of gun ownership and violence, is one of the most divisive issues in the United States. The heart is a traditional, almost trite symbol, often associated with tattoos and classic Americana jewellery.

The gun charm makes a sly, sarcastic statement; combined with the clunky chain, it recalls the classic American 'homeboy' gold chains featured in African-American ghetto culture. The adoption of the 'homeboy' necklace is meant to be typical of some trendsetters, who might emulate that subculture's style without necessarily appreciating the irony implicit in the appropriation.

opposite page A variety of icons and symbols was brainstormed before being shortlisted and developed in the sketchbook. The themes begun in the neckpiece are continued in further pieces designed to make a collection for the fashion market. The price tag charms for the bracelet (top) are engraved with different currencies – American dollars, British pounds, Japanese yen, French francs and Portuguese escudos. The earrings (bottom right) involve a heart and a small bullet, and the brooch (bottom left) features a price tag attached to a little arrow, in a reference to consumerism.

right This neckpiece is stylish and suitably fashionable; yet the references to contemporary culture are provocative.

Shot through the heart

coral and a brooch

back

Ring

back view

Front   Back

Brooch

L6,720,000

¥37,200

695,500,500

£3,055

$1,095

fashion overview

Fashion is often a barometer of society; anything in vogue can be the inspiration for fashion jewellery, from social and spiritual trends to politics.

longevity and transience Fashion jewellery is designed to work parallel with the trends of the catwalk, and therefore tends to be seen as transient. As a type of jewellery, however, it has been around for a long time, but was known more commonly as 'costume' jewellery.

Today, mass-market fashion jewellery is accessible because it is produced in great quantities at low cost, and is therefore relatively cheap to buy. This does not necessarily mean that fashion jewellery is worth less; it need not be lightweight or superficial, and if it is well designed, it need not have a short lifespan because its enduring appeal will, after all, be a matter of taste.

right These witty pins look innocent enough with the cheerful ribbon-topped stoppers; however, the inscriptions reveal a dry humour that dispels the innocent demeanour of the pieces in a flash.

below right The cranium is made into an upbeat motif for fashion jewellery. Delicate bright blue ribbons are threaded through the skull-shaped buckles to make the eye sockets fill with colour.

below left The colour and density of the beads make this necklace a visual treat and a desirable fashion piece that could be used to accentuate the colour in a variety of outfits.

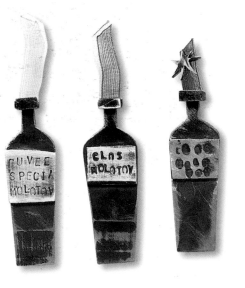

bridging the gap The public appetite for jewellery that is fun and individual appears to be growing more and more insatiable, and designer jewellery for the fashion market is a growing branch of jewellery.

Designer fashion jewellery is also known as 'bridge' jewellery because it bridges the divide between commercial fashion jewellery and fine jewellery. The

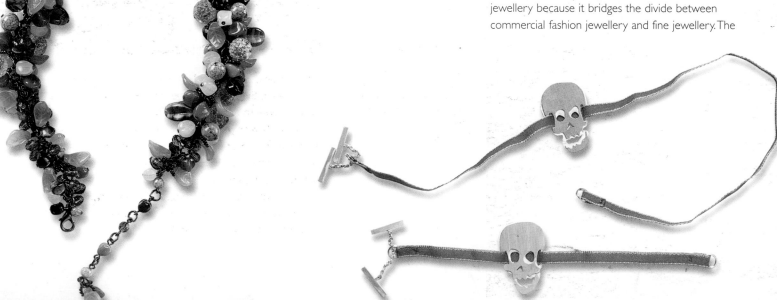

materials and processes used encompass everything from traditional precious metals and gemstones to cheap and cheerful alternatives. These include white metal, plated base metal, plastic, glass beads and almost any material that is exciting, interesting, individual, affordable and distinctive.

Cost is a very important factor in fashion jewellery, which needs to retail at a relatively affordable price. Fashion jewellery that is designer branded tends to be more expensive. Apart from the "snob" factor – people's willingness to pay more money for a piece by

above Light, airy, and attractive, this blue bangle has a clean, modern form, with delicate embedded detail – the perfect accompaniment for a stylish ensemble.

right The simple form of an elliptical epaulette is echoed across the body to make a sash that is held in place by graduated chains. This bold bodypiece makes an eye-catching statement – a refreshing alternative to a pearl choker for a night out on the town.

left Fashion jewellery is often a bit more flamboyant. This pair of impractical glasses and a bizarre bow tie are guaranteed to lend any man an air of distinction and eccentricity.

a well-known designer or brand – it is less likely to be produced in the same quantities as mass-market pieces, and is therefore more expensive to manufacture.

To sell fashion jewellery to retail stores, you will need to create a collection, generally with a minimum of 30 pieces, so that they can make a display of your work that has impact and offers choice to the buyer. The most popular forms are earrings, rings and brooches, and more costly arm- and neckpieces are also needed to attract attention to the work.

fashion jeweller's showcase

> My work is made up of strong, clean, fresh forms inspired by an innovative use of materials and organic structures. The designs are derived from the study of ethnic jewellery forms, natural and manmade materials and strong organic structures. **laura tabor**

summer collection From the original source of inspiration, Laura Tabor developed her ideas using manmade material to try and recreate the aesthetics of the natural source. During the design process, she uncovered and explored hidden qualities in non-precious materials and objects by means of new applications. The contrast of non-precious material with small amounts of precious metals and stones, used in an innovative way, makes the work fresh, fashionable and contemporary. Model making allowed her to test permutations of form, colour, pattern, density of decoration and visual impact in order to create a variety of styles.

When designing a fashion collection, prevalent trends must be taken into consideration. It is important to have an awareness of the seasons so that the designs are centred on a particular colour scheme and style. A good knowledge of fashion is essential if the designer is to create jewellery that is versatile enough to be worn in conjunction with the relevant fashion, cuts of clothes, colour and style.

opposite page Luscious images filled with textures, colours, contrasts and a multitude of form and shape combinations were carefully collated in sketchbooks. In other pieces in the summer collection, Laura intentionally removed colour, giving the forms a different identity and making them eminently suitable for both spring brides and catwalk models. The use of inexpensive materials, such as balloon rubber (for the small rose forms) and acrylic helps to keep costs down.

this page These simple cuffs, which make up part of a fun, feminine summer collection. are made from plastic. Images of roses were printed onto the plastic before it was sprinkled with diamantes.

fine overview

Jewellery made of precious materials, such as gold, platinum and gemstones, is generally described as 'fine'.

value for money Fine jewellery tends to be, or at least appear, more traditional or conventional than other types of jewellery, perhaps because it is the intention that the piece can be worn daily and it is therefore required to deliver value for money. Fine jewellery is often seen as an investment, so the design is likely to be more classical. It may also be contemporary, but not revolutionary, as it will often have to stand the test of time. Although precious metals and gemstones can be recycled, people who are daring enough with their finances to commission truly innovative or outrageous designs are few and far between.

The relative cost of fine jewellery can be prohibitive for the average person. Those who are not deterred are likely to require a piece to be versatile and durable so that they can get as much wear from it as possible. A design brief for fine jewellery might require that the piece be strong enough to withstand daily wear but not appear unnecessarily strong or overtly stalwart.

a token of promise The possibility of owning

right This white and yellow 18-ct gold ring is bezel-set, with diamonds in the undulating folds of the ring face.

below left These two platinum-and-diamond rings are ideally suited to daily wear. The bezel setting chosen for the sapphires is simple yet durable, as it surrounds the stone with a protecting wall of metal. The diamonds are gypsy-set into the shank of the rings so that there is no perceptible setting and therefore nothing to catch on fibres, or accidentally scratch the skin and other surfaces, as can occasionally happen with a claw setting.

right Diamonds and gold are combined in this classical pendant, reminiscent of the Byzantine era. Using 22-ct gold granulation and hand-woven chain, the design and execution of this modern piece evokes the magnificence of an ancient civilisation.

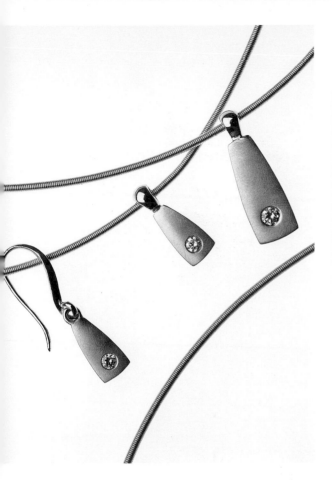

left A suite of 18-ct gold-and-diamond jewellery offers the same form in a variety of sizes and formats – large pendant, small pendant, and earrings. The simplicity of the design is extremely inviting, as it can be worn practically all the time – it is ideal for dressing up jeans, yet formal enough for a visit to the opera.

above Precious jewels need not be overdressed. These sizable diamonds are feature enough, but the gentle, curvaceous texture of the borders frames the diamonds, and at the same time accentuates the play of light on their many faces.

below This unconventional engagement ring uses traditional jewellery materials – diamonds and gold – that are commonly associated with engagement rings. However, with a circle of similar stones around the form, the format is more like that of an eternity ring.

fine jewellery for pure adornment tends to be for the privileged few, since the materials associated with fine jewellery make such extravagance costly. Therefore, pieces of fine jewellery are generally saved up for or purchased by installments, and are usually bought for a special reason or occasion.

A common reason for buying fine jewellery is to mark an engagement – and, along with the wedding band, the stone-set ring is one of the most popular fine jewellery forms. Although a variety of gemstones is used in engagement rings, diamonds are the stone most commonly associated with the engagement ring because they are valuable, and they are also the most durable of the gemstones.

fine case studies

Raised details accentuate form and the design intention; four stones, four children, four decades.

The channel setting makes small diamonds into a bank of stones, heightening their visual impact.

this page For a mother of four the simple format of this 18-ct gold, sapphire and diamond ring is perfect, as the ring is durable and can be worn daily.

Because this ring is invested with such importance, models are made from these drawings and approved by the designer to show the clients before the design is finalised and the piece is made.

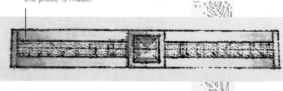

The longevity of precious materials is a key factor in fine jewellery, which may be valued on intrinsic worth alone. However, there is no reason why the design should not be considered as precious as the materials used.

to commemorate and celebrate Often pieces that are intended to be worn daily are commissioned for a specific occasion. The design brief for the piece on this page was for a fine jewellery piece to celebrate the birth of a fourth child, as well as a fortieth birthday. The designer chose the form of an eternity ring, the most appropriate for the concept. The number of stones in the ring is highly symbolic – the four sapphires represent the offspring, and the sum of all the stones is exactly 40. When the house is quiet and the children have left the nest, the ring will be a reminder of the children and a symbol of the love of her spouse, who commissioned the piece.

A final rendering is made from two angles so that the design can be easily understood.

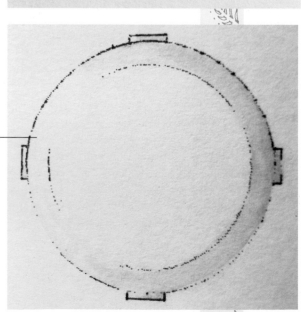

classical splendour Designing specifically around precious materials and unusual gemstones gives this designer all the inspiration they need to spend time and effort on honing surface detail and creating the perfect setting to suit the character of material, form and individual stones. Simplicity and understatement are the key elements of this fine jewellery, and attention to detail and craftsmanship are of paramount importance. The detail, balance, proportion and aesthetic of each piece has been carefully considered so that the classical splendour is enhanced with a unique, individual quality.

Fine jewellery doesn't have to be droll or conventional. The innovative design for this pearl

above A vibrant pink ruby is set with two diamonds in a 22-ct gold ring that is both durable and sophisticated. The crisp lines of a champagne diamond are complemented beautifully by the yellow gold that it is set in, and the gypsy-set white diamonds on the shank.

top left The beaten silver of these graceful ring and bangle forms is lined with 22-ct gold so that they lie softly against the skin. The marriage of the rich, warm yellow and the cool white creates subtle contrast.

left Tiny white diamonds adorn the waist of this beaten 18-ct gold bangle and accentuate a round shank below a sumptuous diamond in a platinum ring. In contrast with the grandeur of the bangle and ring, a pair of simple platinum studs are set with modest square diamonds.

right The traditional pearl necklace is transformed into a piece of contemporaneous design using innovative new technology.

necklace (below) used up-to-date technology called laser welding, which is used in place of conventional soldering. Through this process, the heat that is generated when a joint is made is localised so that delicate, very costly pearls can be incorporated into jewellery that is joined physically rather than mechanically. Normally it would be impossible to physically join metal that is in contact with pearls through soldering, because this would result in the pearls being scorched or burnt.

The designer used platinum and 18-ct gold to make orbital cage forms that hold the pearls while also acting as the integral linking system.

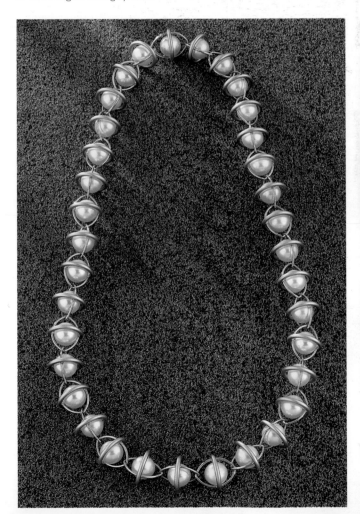

fine jeweller's showcase

"Designing for an important occasion is always enjoyable, however, an engagement ring is especially satisfying and agreeable because it denotes the act of betrothal – the piece is indued with symbolic meaning, transformed into an insignia of a pledge between two people."

elizabeth olver

opposite page Because the ring is to be invested with such importance, both sketches and models were made for approval by the clients before the design was finalised. The settings were made higher than necessary so that they could be lowered, and the valuable diamonds were lightly set as a temporary measure to ensure that they would not be mislaid while the ring was being trialed.

the wardour ring An engagement ring as well as an heirloom, the medieval splendour of Old Wardour Castle – the ancestral home of the bride-to-be – is reflected in the settings, and the union of two families is represented by the inclusion of elements of heraldry from both houses, which are engraved on the shank of the ring.

Resetting is a common practice with gemstones, as they are frequently passed down through the generations of a family. For this piece, three of an original four old-cut diamonds from the groom's family lend themselves to a grand design inspired by architecture and regal finery. The base of the ring has a diamond-set detail that helps to balance the aesthetic of this monumental piece, which is destined to become part of the family's history.

right The finished 18-ct, yellow-gold ring has an old-cut, cushion-shaped diamond that sits resplendent as if it were literally set atop a tower. This is flanked by rose-cut diamonds that are claw-set in handsome forms that resemble coronets.

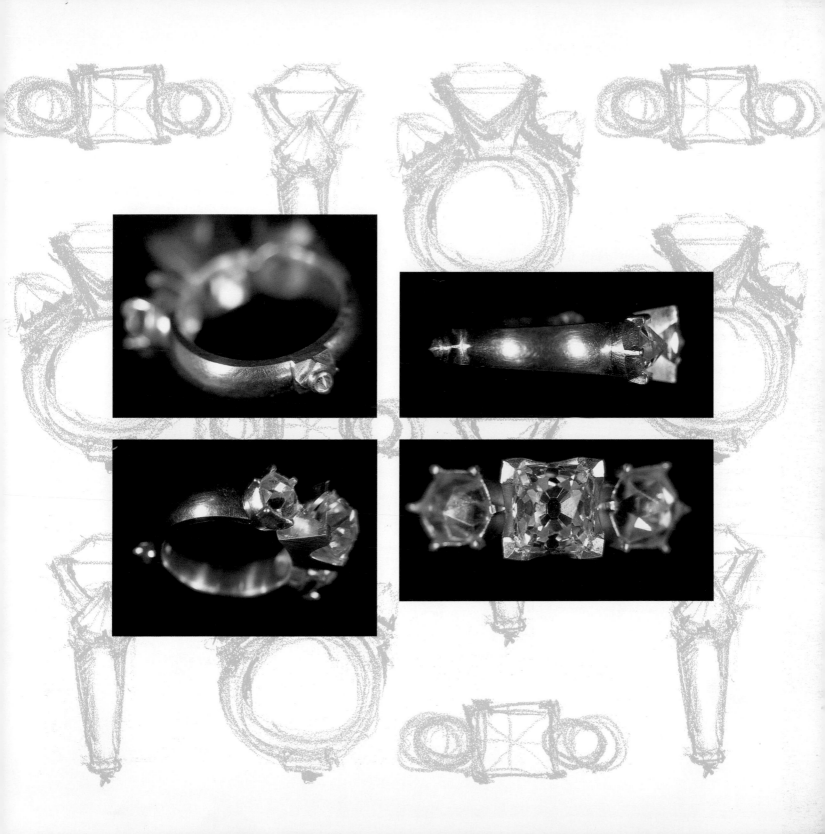

series overview

Making jewellery in a series is a useful way to explore and exploit a theme, material, concept or process. A series can be a succession or set of pieces in which there is a progressive difference that maintains a perceptible link or relationship between the forms.

design development tool Designers often prefer to design single pieces because this allows them to create an individual statement. However, in the making of one piece, a number of ideas may be generated that progress and lead to another piece being conceived. From that, further changes may suggest themselves so that one idea becomes two, then three, and so on.

It is useful to imagine how you can develop a piece into a series, either by embellishing or simplifying it. Take a process that is appropriate for large-scale production, like casting, and a simple flat ring shank, for example; with the addition of detail through a continuous process of mould making, reworking, mould making, re-working, mould making, etc., the form will be altered significantly, stage by stage, and the plain ring shank can be transformed into something entirely different.

right As a group, this series of pins looks almost insect-like. The delicate and beautiful forms are clearly related as a series by the choice of materials. The careful addition of colour is used to help attract attention to the linear forms.

below left In this series of bangles made of tin, delicate surface patterns are created using a variety of subtle shades of precious gold and platinum leaf.

below right These rings were made as vehicles for different forms of food. The same basic formula is used for each one, while the surface shape is modified according to which foodstuff each is supposed to contain.

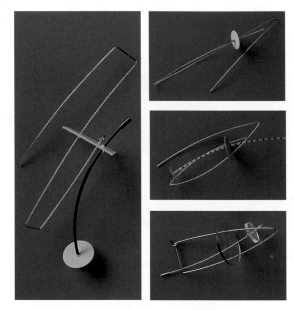

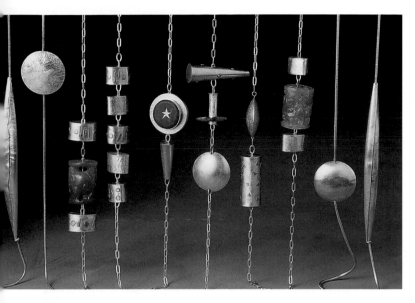

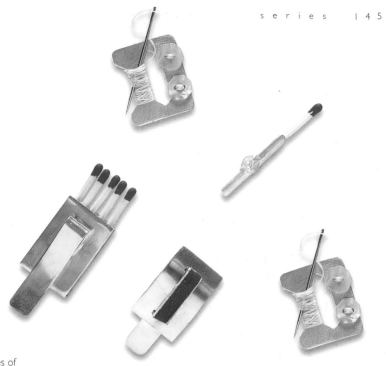

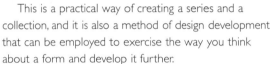

This is a practical way of creating a series and a collection, and it is also a method of design development that can be employed to exercise the way you think about a form and develop it further.

In addition, there will be times when you find that it is difficult to maintain drive and momentum with your work, as things don't always go as planned. As a catalyst for further productivity and inspiration, consider returning to a favourite piece and try to develop the design as if it were a new series.

obsession For some people the need to make a series of pieces appears to be based on a pre-occupation, or even an obsession. This can be great to spur design development, and tends to mean that there is a real connection between the designer and his or her work, fuelling the motivation to carry on designing and working at the bench. The underlying concept creates the link, and it is not uncommon to see a lifetime's work as a series, as often there will be a style thread that connects individual pieces to a larger body of work.

above In this series of neckpieces the suspended forms are varied to change the character of each piece. The choice of form, colour, and texture offers something for everyone – the biggest problem would be choosing only one to take home!

above right These unisex jewellery forms are a clever take on the necessities of a modern lifestyle; the concept of the series is clearly read and acts as the link for the different shapes and contents, connecting the various forms with ease and dexterity.

right The designer can alter the armature that will define the shape of each ring, and then, using a binding technique, join, decorate and relate the rings as a series.

series case studies

'The more the merrier' rings true in the context of series, because the impact of the work is enhanced by quantity. In making a series of pieces you create the opportunity for choice, both for yourself as a designer, and for the user.

interactive series The concept of our lives being predestined is of great interest to the designer of the series of interactive pieces shown here, and humankind's desire to know what that destiny is was the inspiration behind the work; wearers are invited to divine the milestones that will mark the narrative of their lives.

The designer looked at different means of predicting the future in a variety of cultures, and then considered a number of elements in our lives that may be influential and interesting. A different ring for each of these potential momentous events was then devised, and with each piece comes a different interactive method for divulging the fortunes of that life marker.

right Presented in its own box, the divining set looks at select areas of our destiny – how will love treat us? How many children will we have? Will they be male or female? Will we have to carry a burden? Will it be responsibility or disability? Will we live a long or short life?

below These design development drawings give insight into the designer's inspiration for a ring that will divine our life burdens.

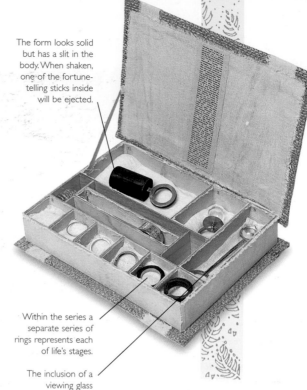

The form looks solid but has a slit in the body. When shaken, one of the fortune-telling sticks inside will be ejected.

Within the series a separate series of rings represents each of life's stages.

The inclusion of a viewing glass connects this ring to the others, which require magnification if their engraved text is to be easily read.

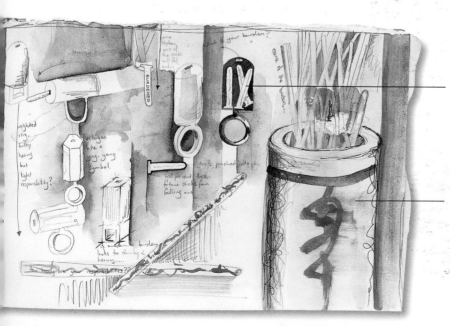

The designer has explored a number of ideas, although not all are realised in the final complete series. This was to be a tab shaken from the container ring form.

The designer has taken inspiration from an oriental means of fortune telling. A bamboo container is full of sticks on which various fortunes are written. When shaken, the container ejects a stick, which is deemed to tell the fortune.

key points

Pieces in a series should maintain a perceptible link between the forms

✳

Series have the potential for greater visual impact, and offer the customer more choices

✳

Returning to a favourite piece to develop it as a series can be a means of building drive and momentum

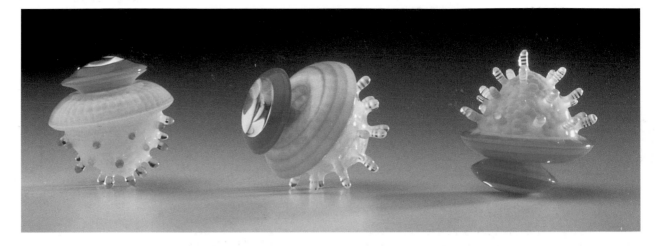

right Individually these spinning brooches may seem diminutive, but when assembled together the playful little characters exude immense charm – and at the same time their visual impact is greatly enhanced.

below Simple geometric forms in a series of rings are used to test mechanisms for changing size. By making quick sketches in metal, mechanisms can be tested with minimal effort.

the sum of its parts

Because a designer is much more likely to be able to draw the eye to a number of related objects than to a single object, the initial visual impact that a series makes is vital. When working on a collection, it is likely that you will create pieces of varying complexity; some of these may be designed as a single momentous statement, while others may be conceived as a series, in which the combinative effect of a number of simple or smaller pieces is designed to make an impact equal to that of a stand-alone statement.

function and aesthetics

A series of forms can be made as a means of developing and testing an idea. For the designer of these rings (left), the object of the exercise was to discover different ways of altering the ring size. By considering a number of mechanisms and translating these into jewellery forms, the potential of the mechanism could be tested. As each form was made, the designer considered other permutations of the mechanism in another form or series of forms.

Within the series, subseries appear in which the designer has varied the mechanism, or the format for the mechanism, to test the aesthetics of each piece in addition to its function.

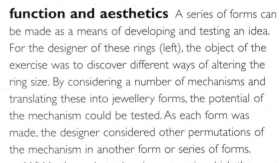

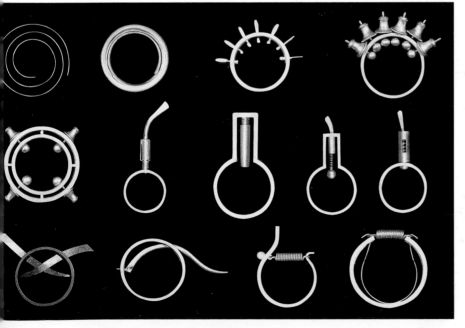

series jeweller's showcase

> ❝ I am not interested in designing single pieces. My intention is to make modern jewellery that will not lose its validity in the future. Some of the rings are designed as sculptural objects that include a riddle; how will this ring be held on the hand? ❞ **angela hübel**

the centre of attention The ring theme imposes the most limits on the free choice of forms. It is a tremendous challenge to find interesting solutions – despite the limitations of the human anatomy. Of all of the parts of the body that can be ornamented, the hand is the one that is the most frequently in motion. This continual motion makes the ring into the 'liveliest' piece of jewellery, one that is always at the centre of attention.

Angela Hübel sets herself the challenge to make contemporary forms – simple, reduced, modern, but not too technical, perfect, or regular – with tiny natural irregularities, like those that exist in the human body. She seeks inspiration through a ceaseless collecting of forms – ideas don't arrive accidentally out of the clear blue sky. The concept for each ring is the result of intense cognitive and experimental work motivated by the sheer pleasure of designing jewellery.

The stimulation lies in a yearning to continue varying a theme until all the possibilities are exhausted and an exquisite series of related forms is created.

opposite In this architecturally inspired series, elegant 18-ct gold rings are constructed to frame or bridge the fingers so that the forms appear almost as one with the hand. As part of the design process, simple drawings explore forms on the finger. The rings are designed so that equal value is placed on ensuring comfort when the form is worn, the formal correctness of the ring as an object, and the harmonious aesthetic interplay between the ring and the hand.

right In this series of 18-ct gold-and-diamond rings, subtle permutations of form and aesthetic challenge the possibilities of the ring form.

sculptural overview

Jewellery is often designed for purely aesthetic reasons, with no greater agenda in mind than adornment. However, many designers consider their work a mouthpiece for jewellery design in the field of fine art. This begs the question: is jewellery-making a design discipline or a fine art discipline? Because of functional requirements, most people see jewellery as design based, but there is no reason it cannot make a fine art statement, especially since its three-dimensional nature enables it to be realised as miniature sculpture.

attention and understanding The
intellectual content, or the concept, is an important aspect of work that is designed both to be viewed as an artwork and also worn on the body as a piece of jewellery. Most designers of sculptural jewellery are interested in making pieces that have a strong impact so that they can attract attention and communicate ideas that might otherwise be overlooked or not considered.

Because sculptural jewellery is generally intended to be thought-provoking, it has a bigger agenda than some other types of jewellery, and tends to be more complex or sophisticated on several levels. There are

above These lively rings have a playful quality that makes them attractive both on and off the body. The clever fitting ensures that the rings maintain their own identity without an obvious reference to jewellery when not being worn.

below left and below Although any one of this set of four rings can be worn, the intention is for them to be displayed together as a sculptural work, as seen in the sketches. Placed above a mirror, the moonstones within the cylinder forms can be seen.

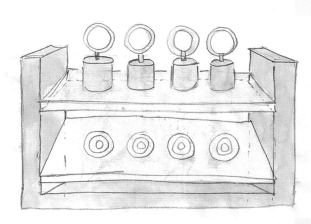

several design devices, beyond shape, form, colour, texture and so on, that can be used to help ensure that the idea is successfully communicated to the viewer. The addition of a title may be enough to help explain the concept, and engaging the viewer or wearer in an interactive process can help reinforce the concept behind the piece.

on and off the body

As with all types of jewellery, sculptural work needs to be carefully designed so that shape, form, colour, texture, emotional impact, function and concept have all been considered. In addition, with sculptural work you need to decide how the piece will function when it is not worn – this is important because the jewellery should be a statement off the body as well as on, and therefore should be considered holistically.

The element that indicates how a piece will function – whether it is a pin, clasp or hole for a finger or arm – is generally less obvious in a sculptural piece than in other forms of jewellery. It is likely that the functional aspect of the design will be integrated with the overall form so that it is not a focal point and is therefore generally less obvious.

above and above left Childhood obsessions were the inspiration for this pair of rings, based on a treasure box and a candy jar. Although they can be worn, they also stand as desirable objects when off the finger.

above right This delicate ring is too delightful to be put away in a box and hidden from view. The glass container acts as a showcase for the fragile, pearl-tipped thorny twig, and the body of the ring is inscribed with the words of a song.

centre right and bottom right In this piece, entitled 'Funeral Feather for Brazil', each leaf-shaped element is inscribed with the name of an endangered species on one side and a tyre track on the other. The number of elements equals the number of endangered species at the time the piece was made. The 'feathers' can be removed from the pin as a species becomes extinct.

sculptural case studies

Designing sculptural jewellery can be intensely personal; it can also be a cathartic process. Sculptural jewellery lends itself well to designs that make a statement that will touch others who have empathy with the ideas, materials, symbolism, or ethos embraced in the design.

childhood remembered For the designer of the piece on this page, feelings of nostalgia and protection toward childhood were the inspiration for a complex piece of sculptural jewellery. Childhood is a special time, and the designer's memories of that time have become particularly precious.

Various materials are contained in the pendant. Slate is a reminder of an affinity with nature that began in the designer's childhood, plaster represents the permanence of memories, and personal objects collected in the past symbolise childhood passions – nature, construction and imagination. The clock dials are symbolic of the passing of time; the button is included to represent something lost that is now useless; and a deliberately ambiguous message written inside is so small that it requires the ring set with a magnifying stone to read it.

this page The delicacy of this intriguing work, comprising two mutually reliant forms, is indicative of the degree of sensitivity felt by the designer toward the objects and ideas that were the inspiration for this sculptural piece.

When closed, the pendant acts as a protective casing for the delicate ring form.

The pendant form opens up to reveal precious treasures.

The magnifying stone is required to explore the conundrums of the pendant.

The button represents something lost that is now useless.

key points

Sculptural jewellery should function both on and off the body

The 'function' may not only be how the piece is worn, but also how it is displayed

The interactive element is a very useful design device for emphasising the concept behind sculptural pieces

right Three 18-ct gold rings become miniature sculptures with a touch of humour – by trying on the rings or playing with them the viewer discovers that the toast pops up, the wine can be uncorked and the fish makes a bid for freedom.

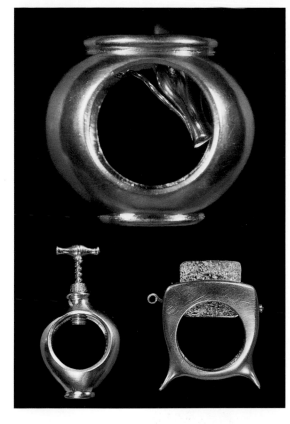

fun and frustration
Another designer has captured the fun and frustration of being a child in a series of rings (left), which takes playful images and ideas and translates them into 'grown-up' materials made through serious craft skill. The frustration of a child who wants to be an adult, wearing mother's perfume, shoes and jewellery, is remembered in these pieces.

These sculptural rings are designed to be changed in size so that they can be passed down through the generations of a family without alteration; even though they don't fit the small fingers of an eager child, they do allow a variety of people of different shapes and sizes to enjoy wearing them. Each of the rings has been designed so that it can stand upright when not worn and be viewed as a small sculptural ornament.

seriously casual jewellery
What happens to a piece of jewellery when it is removed from the body is of particular importance in the armpiece below. Far from being concerned that the silver form be kept safe and sound in a secure box, the designer wanted it to become a piece of sculpture when not worn.

For this reason, the designer covered the back of the silver form with Velcro. The wearer is encouraged to throw the armpiece casually onto a surface on which there is another strip of Velcro, which will hold it in place and thereby transform the armpiece from a jewellery object into an item of spontaneous sculpture.

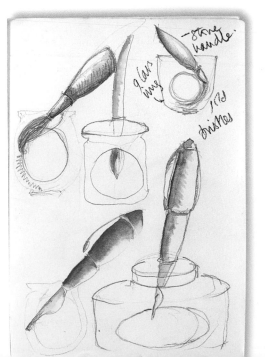

left Pen and ink, a paintbrush, and a pot of water are considered in a series of lively sketches as options for sculptural rings to please the eye, both off the finger as well as on it.

right This simple armpiece was first handworked using an organic fabrication process in the relatively pure metal, Britannia silver. It was then backed with the manmade material Velcro as a contrast to the naturally evolved form. This piece of jewellery was designed to be a work of art both on and off the body.

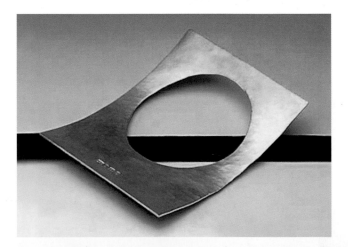

sculptural jeweller's showcase

" I am very interested in "unrealized" jewellery that does not necessarily have to be worn. Much of my work is concerned with the struggle to understand everyday life – this piece is concerned with the weight of one's conscience, and relates to experiences from my childhood. "

zoe arnold

confession box The theme of this monumental sculptural piece is conscience, represented here as a tree – a thing of beauty that has many facets and is also widely known as a symbol of knowledge. Beneath the tree is a glass container that contains a seed and a rusty ball. The seed represents potential – if you ignore your conscience, it becomes crushed and cannot flourish or grow, just as if you disregard the seed, it will never develop into a plant. The ring is designed so that when it is worn the seed will be damaged; it is up to the owner to decide whether or not to wear the piece. Indeed, it is not a piece that is intended to be worn – it is more a reminder of things that play on the conscience than a functional piece of jewellery.

The 'Confession Box' also includes various other forms, including a ring inscribed with a Maori proverb, a fragile bird ring, an egg form made of the shell of a small bird that perished in the designer's garden and a cluster of small stick men, derived from the saying: 'conscience has a thousand witnesses'.

right The fragile forms that make up this piece are entombed in a heavy concrete box that, when closed, offers but a glimpse of its contents. In the same way as a conversation can promote insight, by examining this piece we are invited to learn a little of the burden of conscience.

opposite page A pair of rings that examines the weight of relationships. These forms function as sculpture much more obviously than they do as pieces that can be worn as jewellery. The fate of an egg is described in the sketches below. These were part of the design development process for 'Confession Box'. Eggs are a symbol of life, growth and potential, and the designer's interest in them stems in part from the feelings of guilt she has for having eaten eggs.

glossary

Alloy A mixture of two or more metals.

Aluminium A lightweight, bluish silver-white malleable, ductile metal.

Anodising A process for changing the surface colour of metals, most commonly aluminium and titanium, using an electric current.

Base metal Non precious metals such as aluminium, brass, copper, gilding metal, nickel, pewter, steel and titanium.

Bezel The metal rim in which a stone is set.

Binding wire Steel wire that is used to secure or bind work during the soldering process.

Cabochon A gemstone that has been cut in a convex form and has a smooth, rounded surface.

CAD Computer aided design.

Carnelian A quartz stone that is generally red in colour.

Casting A means of reproducing three-dimensional forms in metal by pouring the metal into a hollow form made from a variety of media such as sand, cuttlefish and plaster.

Casting master A master pattern or form that can be used to make a mould for casting in bronze, silver, gold or platinum.

Catch A fastening that can be opened and closed and which is used to secure necklaces, bracelets and chains.

Channel setting A means of setting stones between two walls of metal formed like a gutter.

Cold etching The controlled corrosion of a surface using cold acids to create decorative or textured patterns.

Cutting list A list of materials used in making a piece of jewellery, including dimensions and quantities, as a way to record the materials required.

Doming A process by which metal is formed into domes using metal formers.

Ductile A term used to describe a material that is yielding or pliable.

Electroforming A process used to deposit a lightweight, hard skin of metal onto a form, partially or completely covering its surface.

Equilateral triangle A triangle with three equal sides.

Etch resist Used to protect or mask areas that are not to be etched so that patterns and detail can be formed.

Etching The controlled corrosion of a surface using acids to create decorative or textured patterns.

Eternity ring A ring set with stones all the way around that is given to mark the birth of a first child.

Facets A term used to describe a gemstone that has been cut so that its form is covered in small, polished flat surfaces.

Fastenings Catches, fittings, or findings used to secure two parts such as the ends of a necklace or bracelet.

Filing A process of removing a layer of material by pushing a cutting face over the surface

Finish The final surface treatment of a piece.

Fold forming A process where a folded sheet is forged to create a three-dimensional, curvaceous form.

Former A structure, generally made of steel, used to support metal while it is being formed.

Gemstones The precious and semiprecious stones used in jewellery

Gilded Gold plated.

Isosceles triangle A triangle with two sides of equal length.

Laser cutting A process for the controlled and accurate cutting of material such as sheet metal and Perspex by laser.

Laser welding A process of joining two materials by the application of localised heat using a laser.

Lathe A tool for cutting a rotating object with accuracy.

Malleable A term used to describe a material that can be readily formed or rolled.

Maquette A small model, usually made of wax or clay, of an object that is to be made in a larger scale.

Mill pressing A process for transferring a pattern or texture onto sheet metal by passing it through rolling mills with paper or other materials.

Mokumé gane A process where layers of metal are fused together to make a mokumé laminate. A pattern is made by deforming or cutting into the surface, filing back and rolling flush the layers of metal exposed by filing.

Noble metal Metals that do not readily tarnish when exposed to air such as silver, gold and platinum; the opposite of base metal.

Palladium A dark gray metal, rather like platinum, that is occasionally used in jewellery making.

Patination A process for colouring metals through exposure to a variety of chemicals.

Perspex A form of clear or coloured thermoplastic resin that can be bought in a variety of formats including sheet and rod.

Photoetching A form of etching that uses ultraviolet light to expose artwork on to sensitised metal sheets that are then etched.

Pickling A process that uses a chemical solution to remove the black oxide layer that results from heating and soldering.

Piercing The process of creating sheet metal in which spaces have been cut away to make an ornamental lace-like pattern. Also know as 'fretwork'.

Plastic A man-made material that can be molded such as Perspex sheet and embedding and casting resins.

Plate A fine covering of metal deposited on another metal surface by an electronic current.

Precious A term used to describe diamonds, sapphires, rubies and emeralds when referring to stones or gold, silver and platinum when referring to metals.

Pressing A process used to produce hollow sheet forms.

Profile The outline of an object that defines its shape.

Soldering A process for joining two pieces of metal using an alloy called solder, which melts at a low temperature and cools to form a joint.

Templates A pattern, model, or mould shaped to a required outline and used as a guide for marking and cutting.

Titanium A hard lightweight, gray material that can be coloured by anodising to produce a spectrum of bright colours.

Tooling The making and setting up of tools for production.

White metal A relatively heavy, gray tin-based metal alloy with a very low melting point; often used in mass-market jewellery.

index

Numbers in *italics* refer
to captions

Abrams, Whitney 126
abstract forms *31*,
  108–13
acrylic 70, 93
all, anodised 93, *93*
amulets 123
armpieces 58, *58*, *109*,
  135, 153, *153*
Arnold, Zoe 154
'At night the mountain
  glows red'
  (enamelling) *69*
bangles: agate 87
  'container' *62*
  fashion *135*
  geometric *104*
  gold and diamond
    141
  key-shaped *61*
  paper 54, 87, *87*
  ribbon 57, *57*
  saddle 58, *58*
  series *144*
  silver: and gold *141*;
    and paper *67*; and
    ribbon 86, *87*
beads 66, *134*, 135
body language 114, *114*
bodypiece *135*
  'Dancers' 116, *116*
Bone, Elizabeth 106
bracelets 45, 100–1, *101*
  buckle *128*
  price tag *132*
  silver 57, *57*; annealed
    64

brooches 26, 115
  box 125, *125*
  cross 130, *130*
  'Dogs in Space' 78
  drawings of 24, *48*
  fashion 135
  feather 66
  figurative *114*
  gold-leaf *104*
  'Jewels, The' 77
  leather *58*
  'Love Kit' 123
  'Mask' *114*
  'Menagerie à Trois' 77
  mokumé gane 44, *48*,
    61, *91* and
    neckpiece, linked
    33
  organic 100–1, *100*,
    101
  pins for 80, *81*
  pod *102*
  price tag *132*
  related *69*
  silver *80*; and acrylic
    81
  spider and web *109*
  spinning *147*
  textured *62*
colour 24, 25, 66–71, 82,
  93
colour studies 68, *68*
commemorative pieces
  120, *120*, 126, *126*
'Communication
  Accessory' *82*
computer, use of 110
concept 34–5, 36, 37
'Confession Box' 154

container pieces 82, *82*
contour lines 56, *56*
cross motif 23, 120, *120*,
  129, 130–1, *130*, *131*
'Crossing'
  (commemorative
  piece) 120, *120*
crystals 52, 85
cuffs, plastic *136*
Cunningham, Jack 120

'Dancers' bodypiece 116,
  116
design brief 32–3
design elements 24, 25
design development
  22–5, 99
designer jewellery 134–5
diamonds 32, 99, 139,
  142
Djorup, Mikala 64
'Dogs in Space' theme
  78, *78*
'Don't Box Me In'
  earrings 131, *131*
drawing 10–11
  life 11, *11*, 116
  technical *10*, 11
  three-dimensional 55

earpiece *116*
earrings: commemorative
  120, *120*
  cross 131, *131*
  'Don't Box Me In\
    131, *131*
  fashion 69, 135
  gold *19*
  hair *122*

heart and bullet *132*
  'Pressure Points' 74
  tinplate 92, *92*
emotion 24, 25, 76–9,
  120
enamel/enamelling 19, 69,
  69, 118
'Eternal Life' 35
'Eyespy' ring 74

fabrication 44–5
fashion pieces 134–7
feathers 66, 99
figurative pieces 114–17
fine jewellery 138–43
fish motif 77, 109, 131,
  131
five senses 24, 25, 72–5
form 24, 25, 54–9, 64
function 24, 25, 80–3
'Funeral Feather for
  Brazil' pin *151*

gemstones 135, 138, 139
  reset 142
  unusual 141
'Genesis' neckpiece 112,
  112
geometric forms 104–7
Gilmour, Beth 58
gold 66, 84, 85, 131, 138,
  141
gold leaf 92
Graveson, Sarah 78

hair 99, *122*, 123, 126,
  126
'Haley Toesis' pin 78
'Heartsick for America'

(neckpiece) 132, *132*
Hills, Catherine 112
'Holding Noise' rings 74
house, gold and enamel
  118
Hübel, Angela 148
humour 77

icons 128–33
inspiration 26–9, 34, 36,
  60, 92, 98–9, 100, *119*,
  134, *151*
interactive pieces 35, 119,
  146
internet 39

jade 85
'Jewels, The' brooch 77

'Key to Chastity, The'
  ring-cum-pendant 32
kinetic designs 94, *94*
Kulagowski, Yvonne 116

lacquer *41*, 44, 63, 90
lateral thinking 23
'Lemon Sunshine'
  pendant 74
lemons: research into *38*
  studies of *48*
Lorinczi, Stacey 132

Marshall, Sarah May 82
'Mask' brooch *114*
materials 24, 25, 84–9
  alternative 86–7
  natural 35, 85, 100
'Menagerie à Trois'
  (brooch) 77

models/model-making 18, 42–3, *42, 43*, 50, *51*, 56, 78, *102*, 116, *140, 142*

mokumé gane 44, 48, 61, 90, *90*

'Moon, The' *44*

movement 57, 70

narrative pieces 112, 118–21

necklaces: leather 58
pearl 141, *141*
resin 67
silver and plastic 64
see also neckpieces

neckpieces 69
and brooch, linked *33*
fashion 135
'Genesis' 112, *112*
'Heartsick for America' 132, *132*
multimedia *19*
paper cord 61, 87, *87*
'Princess' 52, *52*
series *145*
shakudo 88
silver *88*; annealed 64
tendril 102, *102*
'Time Signals II' 106, *106*
wood 88

negative space 51, 58

Olver, Elizabeth 142
opals 85
organic forms 67, 98–103, 104

paper 40, 41, 54, 84, 86, *86, 87*

patination *61*, 102
Paxon, Adam 70
pearls 84, 85, *85*, 131, *131*
pendants: butterfly *98*
chalcedony and crystal *52*
childhood memories 152, *152*
diamond *138*
fossil 100, *100*
heart and poem *128*
interactive 35
lemon 100, *100*
'Lemon Sunshine' 74
resin 54
silver 66, 72
spider 76
perfume 72, 74
Perspex 116, *116*
pewter, sand-cast 93
pill box, silver 82, *82*
pins 44
fashion *134*
'Haley Toesis' 78
series *144*
silver *119*; and paper 86, *86*
spider *111*
plastic 66, 84, 135
platinum 84, 92, 138, 141
Potter, Suzanne 74
'Pressure Points' earrings 74
pricing 45
'Princess' neckpiece 52, *52*
processes 24, 25, 90–5, 102
production 45

research 38–9
ring-cum-pendant 32
ring-within-brooch 125, *125*
rings: abstract *108, 109*
acrylic 99
aquamarine 99
bar 72
candle 33
diamond 32, 105, *138*, 141
divining 146, *146*
double 105
engagement 139, *139*, 142, *142*
eternity 140, *140*
'Eyespy' 74
fashion 135
food 72, 144
geometric *104, 105*
gold 84
graduation 122–3
'Holding Noise' 74
kinetic 94
lacquer 63
moonstone 88, *88*, 150
mourning 126, *126*
pearl 85, 99
quail's egg 86, 87
'Rotate Galaxy' 63
sapphire *138*
sculptural 153, *153*
seed 154
series 23, 145, *147*, *147, 148, 148*
signet 123, *123*
silver 27, 55, 94, 99, *124*; and gold *141*
size alteration 80, *109*, *147, 147*

teeth *122*
temptation 73
textured 63
two-part 54
twig and glass *151*
'We worship at the altar of mammon' 32
white flower 64, *64*
'Rotate Galaxy' ring 63

samples 18, *19*, 22, 40–1, *40, 41*, 92
sapphires 140
Sauer, Jenny 52
sculptural pieces 150–5
seeds 66, 82, 100, 154
series jewellery 144–9
shape 24, 25, 48–53
shells 39, 99
sketches of *31*
silver 49, 66, 85, 88, 100, 102
annealed 64
Britannia *153*
brushed 112
combined with alternative materials 86–7
hammered 63
knitted *91*
oxidised *112*
sketching/sketchbooks 11, 12–13, 15, 16, 30–1, 41, 116
sound, use of 62, 64, 73
spider graph 37, *37*
spider motif 76, *76*, 110, *111*
steel 52, 125
suite of jewellery *139*

'Sun and Moon' arm-cum-neck-cum-ankle pieces *104*
symbolic pieces 122–7
symbols/symbolism 37, 100, 120, *120*
religious 123, *129*, 129, 154, *154*
see also icons, symbolic pieces

Tabor, Laura 136
talismans 123
technical journal 16–17, 41
test pieces 40–1
teeth 99, *122*, 123
texture 24, 25, 60–5
tin/tinplate 84, 85, 92, *92*
'Time Signals II' neckpiece 106, *106*
titanium 44, 66

Velcro *81*, 153, *153*
Vilhena, Manuel 88
visual journal 14–15

'We worship at the altar of mammon' ring *32*
wedding band 122, 139
Wells, Paul 102
wire 93
forms 55
models 90
wrap-around ring-to-brooch 70, *70*

Yokoyama, Tomomi 94

credits

Quarto would like to thank and acknowledge the following for supplying pictures reproduced in this book:

Key: b = bottom, t = top, c = centre, l = left, r = right.

Whitney Abrams 122bl, 126/127 all, 129tl, 131tl/cl, 138br (Photographer: Ralph Gabriner), **Eun An** 34bl; 34bc/br (Photographer: Graham Murrell), **Zoe Arnold** 13tl, 15tr/cr, 22bl, 24tr, 30bl, 37tl, 42bl, 125tl/tr, 154 all, 155br/bl; 125br (Photographer: Graham Murrell); 155t (Photographer: Elizabeth Olver), **Malcolm Betts** 141tl/tc/cl (Photographer: Graham Murrell), **Elizabeth Bone** 106/107 all (Photographer: Norman Hollands, C.A.D. work: Andrew Bardill), **Jessica Briggs** 18tr, 42t, 55tr, 56tr, **Elizabeth Caldwell** 15tl, **Jennifer Caldwell** 10br, 13bl/br, 19cr, 30br, 101 all, **Elizabeth Callinocos** 35tl/tc, 49tl, **Kuo-Jen Chen** 11tl, 20ct, 41c, 44bl, 63bl, 66cr, 85br, 90r, 104tr; **Barbara Christie** 10bl, 19tr, 23tr, 97, 115, tl/tc, 119bl, 128br, 131br/c, 145tl (Photographer: Joël Degan), **Kimmie Chui** 151tr (Photographer: Graham Murrell), **Kirsten Clausager** 20t, 27bl/bc (Photographer: Ole Akhoj), **Cox & Power** 105br (Photographer: Tim Kent), **Jacqueline Cullen** 129tr; 151cr/br (Photographer: Graham Murrell), **Jack Cunningham** 20b, 24c, 26c/tc/tr, 29br, 30tr, 34tr, 77cl, 100 all, 114br, 120/121 all, 123tr/c, 128cr, 130 all, **Mikala Djorup** 41br, 64 all, 84tr, 98tr/c, **Dower & Hall** 138bl, 139tl, **Martina Fabian** 31bl, 63br, **Heather Fahy** 69tr/cr (Photographer: Graham Murrell), **Emma Farquharson** 10tr/cr, 31br, 49tr, 119cl; 49br, 104br, 110cl, 119tl, 145br (Photographer: Joël Degan), **Ian Ferguson** 20cb, 44c, 48tr/cr/br, 61br; 93tr/cr/br (Photographer: Terence Bogue), **Anne Finlay** 81tl, 144tr, Shelby Ferris Fitzpatrick 27tl/tr; 72br, 144br; 72tr (Photographer: Mike Blissett), **Beth Gilmour** 58/59 all, 86tl; 59bl/br (Photographer: Elizabeth Olver), **Sarah Graveson** 31tc, 40tr, 78/79 all, 93 all, 114tr, 115tr/cr/br, **Castello Hansen** 81bl, 104bl, **Joanne Haywood** 85tl, 144br; 92 all (Photographer: Elizabeth Olver), **Katharine Haywood** 80tr, **Catherine Hills** 112/113 all (Photographer: Norman Hollands), **Dorothy Hogg** 41tl; 18bl, 21 all, 22tl (Photographer: L.L. Maccoll); 72bl (Photographer: John K. McGregor), **Angela Hübel** 45tl, 84c/cr (Photographer: George Meister); 85tr (Photographer: Eva Jünger); 148/149 all (Photographer: Mathias Hoffmann), **Fleur Klinkers** 66bl/bc (Photographer: Graham Murrell), **Masami Kobayashi** 151tl (Photographer: Graham Murrell), **Yvonne Kulagowski** 11br, 31tl, 116/117 all (Photographer: Alasdair Foster), **Dieter Lorenz** 29tr, 87tl, **Stacey Lorinczi** 36br, 145tr; 132/133 all (Photographer: Elizabeth Olver), **Alice Magnin** 119br/bc, 128t, 134br/tr, **Sarah May Marshall** 39tl; 36bl, 82/83 all

(Photographer: David Turner), **Hannah Martin** 57br/bl, 62cr, **Noriko Matsumoto** 43tr, 124 all; 55br (Photographer: Graham Murrell), **Joanne McDonald** 45tc (Photographer: Graham Murrell), **Sarah Meanley** 11bl, **Francais Montague** 134bl, **Kathie Murphy** 51br, 54bc, 67tl, 133tl, **Monmo Nagai** 133bl (Photographer: Graham Murrell), **Yoshiko Nishina** 14b; 105tl (Photographer: Graham Murrell), **Angela O'Kelly** 28bl, 40bl, 54cl, 61tc, 67tr, 87tr/br (Photographer: Graham Murrell), **Hiroko Okuzawa** 11tr, 15br, 38tr, 39bl, 43bl/br, 109tl, **Elizabeth Olver** 11cr, 12bl, 17br, 22br, 23bl, 25 all, 26b, 32bl/tr, 35br/bc, 50cr/br, 51tl/tr/bl, 54tr/tc, 69bl, 73bl/tc/tr, 77tr, 80bl/br, 84bl/br, 98bl, 109cl, 114br, 123bl, 139br/tr, 140tl/br/cr, 142/143 all, 147b, 153bl/tc, **Peter Page** 118br/tr, 138tr (Photographer: Llewellyn Robin), **Adam Paxon** 19bl, 41cr, 70/71 all, 99tl, 108tr, 147t, 150tr (Photographer: Graham Lees), **Marie Platteau** 55tl, 77tl, 90bl, 91tl, **Suzanne M. Potter** 62tl/bc, 74/75 all, **Simon Ralph** 81br, 153br, **Tom Rucker** 44tr, 141br (Photographer: K. Gâbler), **Jennifer Sauer** 17tl/cl, 38cr/b, 45br/bl, 48bl, 52/53 all, 56br, 110tr/cr/br (Photographer: H. Becker), **Vannetta Seecharran** 57tr/c, 63tr, 86c, **Carla Shanks** 37br; 98br (Photographer: Graham Murrell), **Zara Simon** 133tr (Photographer: Graham Murrell), **Emily Smith** 33br (Photographer: Graham Murrell), **Lila Stern-Shewry** 18tc, 99br; 109br (Photographer: Aliki Sapountzi), **Robyn Stevens** 86br, **Ai Suzuki** 33tl/tr (photographer: Graham Murrell), **Laura Tabor** 12tr, 39tr, 42cr, 66tr, 108bl/br; 136/137 all, **Simon Hicks** 105tr (Photographer: Graham Murrell), **Kyoko Urino** 35tr, 67bc (Photographer: Kuni Yasu), **Manuel Vilhena** 12cr, 24bl, 28tr, 88/89 all, 129bc, 150bl/br, **Paul Wells** 102/103 all, **Kirstie Wilson** 13bc, 16tr/bl/br, 14tr/cr, 29bl, 36tr, 60tr/bl/br, 68tr/bc, 69br; 152 all (Photographer: Graham Murrell), **Franky Wongkar** 23tl, 146bl/tr; 61cl/bl (Photographer: Graham Murrell), **Tomomi Yokoyama** 94/95 all (Photographer: Elizabeth Olver), **Anastasia Young** 24br, 40cr/bcr/br, 76 all, 111 all, 118bl, 122tr/tc/cr/c (Photographer: Graham Murrell).

All other photographs and illustrations are the copyright of Quarto. While every effort has been made to credit contributors, we apologise in advance if there have been any omissions or errors

The author would like to thank Miles, Beth and Penge for their infinite patience and unerring faith, and Yvonne Kulagowski for her help, encouragement and tireless support.